ONE GOD IN TRINITY

ONE GOD
IN
TRINITY

EDITED BY
PETER TOON
JAMES D. SPICELAND

CORNERSTONE BOOKS
WESTCHESTER, ILLINOIS

One God in Trinity
Copyright © Samuel Bagster & Sons Ltd. 1980
First Published 1980

Library of Congress Catalog Card Number 79-57395
ISBN 0-89107-187-3

Published simultaneously by Samuel Bagster & Sons in Great Britain
and by Cornerstone Books in the United States of America, 1980

Cornerstone Books
Westchester, Illinois

Printed in Great Britain

Preface

The origin of this book is to be traced to the conference of the historical theology group of the British Tyndale Fellowship held at Durham in 1978. Most of the chapters originated as papers given there.

It is a particular pleasure for us to offer the Christian reader a book on the primary dogma of Christianity which is written by men from five countries. Surely international co-operation in the exposition and defence of the Faith is a good thing.

Furthermore, the authors reflect various traditions of christian understanding. The Church of England and the Church of Scotland are represented and they are joined by a Roman Catholic and Free Churchmen from Britain and by Presbyterians from the USA.

We are grateful to all the contributors for their readiness to join in this symposium and we thank the editors of the *Scottish Journal of Theology* for permission to reprint Dr Kaiser's article which he has updated.

PETER TOON   JAMES D. SPICELAND

Contents

Contributors

RICHARD BAUCKHAM teaches the history of christian thought in the University of Manchester. He has a doctorate from Cambridge and is the author of *Tudor Apocalypse* (Appleford, Abingdon, 1979).

GERALD LEWIS BRAY, a Canadian, has doctorates from the Sorbonne and Cambridge. He is the author of *Holiness and the Will of God: Perspectives on the theology of Tertullian* (London, 1979). He is an Anglican priest at present serving in east London.

BRIAN HEBBLETHWAITE teaches philosophy of religion at Cambridge where he is a Fellow of Queens' College. He is the author of *Evil, Suffering and Religion* (London, 1976).

ALASDAIR HERON teaches dogmatics in New College, Edinburgh, has a doctorate from Tübingen, and is an editor of the *Scottish Journal of Theology*.

CHRISTOPHER B. KAISER teaches systematic theology at Western Theological Seminary, Holland, Michigan. He has doctorates in science and theology.

BRUCE KAYE, an Australian, is senior tutor of St John's College, Durham. He has a doctorate from the University of Basel and is the author of *The Supernatural in the New Testament* (London, 1977).

HUGO MEYNELL is a Roman Catholic layman. He teaches philosophy of religion in the University of Leeds, has a doctorate from Cambridge and is the author of *An Introduction to the Philosophy of Bernard Lonergan* (London, 1976).

Contributors

ROGER NICOLE is Swiss by birth and teaches systematic theology at Gordon Conwell Seminary, South Hamilton, Massachusetts. He has had a distinguished teaching career and is the oldest contributor.

RICHARD ROBERTS teaches systematic theology in the University of Durham and has a doctorate from Edinburgh.

JAMES SPICELAND teaches philosophy of religion at Western Kentucky University. An American citizen, he took his doctorate at Exeter University in England.

PETER TOON teaches Christian doctrine in Oak Hill Anglican Theological College, London. He has a doctorate from Oxford and his two most recent books are *The Development of Doctrine in the Church* (Grand Rapids, Michigan, 1979) and *Evangelical Theology, 1833–1856: A Response to Tractarianism* (London, 1979).

Introduction

All major christian denominations affirm in their Confessions of Faith that they accept the doctrine of the Trinity. Yet few of their preachers or teachers actually proclaim this belief in sermons. Often the only occasion when the doctrine is explained is when candidates are being prepared for full membership of the local congregation. Having noted this, we must add that where a set liturgy or a fixed order of service is used then there is usually a trinitarian structure to the theology of the service. This is true, for example, of the Anglican service of Holy Communion. However, despite the privileged position of this doctrine in both Confession and Liturgy there seems to be a lack of confidence in it today. The reasons for this may be traced to both the academic and the parish levels.

The scholar naturally wants to be seen to be logical, rational and scientific in his theological statements. But this approach does not easily produce the doctrine that God is One and One in Three. It more easily lends itself to the development of unitarianism if not subject to Revelation.

At the parish level there is a general feeling that the Trinity is both difficult and unimportant. Where a creed is recited it is often done without reflection on its meaning. It is claimed that to have faith in Jesus and to love one's neighbour is what Christianity is all about. The emphasis is on the experiential and the practical and there is fear of the cerebral. Committed Christians do not appear (or are not helped) to interpret their experience of God in a trinitarian manner – and this, despite the uses of 'the grace' of 2 Corinthians 13.14. Certainly there is prayer to the Father and there is belief in the leading and filling of the Holy Spirit, but most Christians appear not to integrate their experience and knowledge of God the Father, Son and Holy Spirit. In fact, on the surface it seems that many Christians get on well without the doctrine of the Trinity.

This book is intended primarily for those who are familiar with the outlines of the traditional, orthodox doctrine of the Trinity as contained in the Nicene and Athanasian Creeds. To refresh the memory Dr Nicole carefully explains the orthodox doctrine in the first chapter.

The purpose of this book is to commend the orthodox doctrine as being more faithful to the biblical witness than either unitarianism or binitarianism. Within this broad purpose there are various other objectives. Aspects of the doctrine which are in current debate are examined – e.g. the biblical witness, the patristic development and the *filioque* clause. Then, for those who know the writings of R. Otto or M. Eliade or I. T. Ramsey, an attempt is made to show what empirical grounds could conceivably count as evidence in favour of trinitarianism in contrast to, say, modalism. Thirdly, the contributions of two great teachers of the orthodox dogma are briefly examined – Karl Barth and Bernard Lonergan. It is hoped that the reader will go on to read these men for himself. Finally, the contributions of several modern theologians who either affirm the doctrine of the Trinity in a novel way or deny it on supposed biblical or rational grounds are noticed. Again it is hoped that the reader will go on to read these authors in order to know how at least some in the Christian Church are thinking.

For those who wish to read a history of the doctrine of the Trinity E. J. Fortman, *The Triune God: A Historical Study of the*

Doctrine of the Trinity (1972) is useful. It is not our intention to repeat what this book and earlier ones contain. We shall be content if we encourage the reader to think deeply about this doctrine, with its theological, practical and liturgical implications. And we shall be most happy if our symposium proves as useful as that on this topic edited by A. E. J. Rawlinson in 1928 and entitled *Essays on the Trinity and the Incarnation*.

Oak Hill College   PETER TOON
London

CHAPTER ONE

The Meaning of the Trinity

The christian Church readily acknowledges that the doctrine of the Trinity is a great mystery which has often been viewed as a stumbling block, an obstacle in the path of those who would embrace the christian faith, and a teaching so flawed by irrationality as to make it unacceptable to thinking minds. It is a major point of disagreement between Christianity and certain non-christian religions, even those which, like Judaism and Islam, are ready to share a high degree of reverence for at least some portions of the Holy Scripture. A number of sects of Christendom have also found it desirable to repudiate the doctrine of the Trinity, and from within the ranks of the Church there have been questions about it and sometimes even attacks against it. It is therefore very important to define carefully the nature of the biblically-based, orthodox view of the Trinity and to assess the impact of that view on the whole body of the christian faith.

I. DEFINITION

The christian doctrine of the Trinity may conveniently be defined in three simple propositions, all three of which are concurrently affirmed.

1) There is one God and one only.
2) This God exists eternally in three distinct persons: the Father, the Son and the Holy Spirit.

3) These three are fully equal in every divine perfection. They possess alike the fullness of the divine essence.

It is the christian distinctive to affirm these three simultaneously. In fact, the most dangerous distortions that challenge the doctrine of the Trinity do affirm two out of the three and deny the third.

A. *Modalism* affirms that there is one God and that Father, Son, and Holy Spirit possess alike the fullness of the divine essence. It denies that God *eternally* exists in three persons. Rather it views the three as successive manifestations of one and the same person: God variously presented as Father or as Son or as Holy Spirit. Of course, this view is confronted by an immense problem in the many passages, particularly in the New Testament, where two or three persons of the Godhead are simultaneously present in the same incident. A good case in point might be the baptism of Jesus, described in Matthew 4 and Luke 4. There we have the Son who received baptism, the Father who speaks from heaven, and the Holy Spirit who descends like a dove. Other examples would not be hard to find. The very terms 'Father' and 'Son' imply a correlation which excludes unipersonality. In the earnest desire for stressing unity the modalist has done great disservice to the personal distinctions within the Godhead. The modalistic approach has been espoused by men of great intellectual power (Swedenborg, Schleiermacher, etc.) and appears to be perennially attractive to speculative thinkers.

B. *Subordinationism* affirms that there is one God but that three essentially separate persons must be considered when discussing our knowledge of God and of his relation to the world. What appears at variance with the Scripture is the proposition that the three – Father, Son, and Holy Spirit –

do not possess alike the divine essence but that they form a hierarchy. Thus the claim of Jesus Christ to deity appears toned down and so is the deity of the Holy Spirit. Inasmuch as all three are to receive divine honours, there is here a very dangerous trend toward polytheism. An alternative consists in reducing Jesus Christ to the level of a mere man and in viewing the Holy Spirit as an influence, an expression of the person of the Father. Here obviously one is at great variance with the biblical representation. It is nevertheless in this category that the most common forms of Antitrinitarianism can be classified. Arianism is the name generally used for this approach when conjoined with a recognition of high supernatural features in Jesus Christ.

c. *Tritheism* at another extreme asserts the eternal existence of the three and their full equality but it denies the monotheistic doctrine of the uniqueness of God. On this account it could never be expected that tritheism would receive acceptance in the Church, since monotheism is deeply implanted in Scripture from Genesis to Revelation.

This situation may be depicted in the following diagram, where each side of the triangle represents one of the three propositional truths to be received. The orthodox view, represented by an inscribed circle, has a firm hold on each of the three great truths. The summits mark the respective positions of heterodox groups in which only two of the three truths are received and the third one is denied. It must be emphasised that this diagram does not constitute a schematic representation of the being of God; it is rather a diagram of the relationships between the trinitarian view and other positions.

This diagram brings to light in a convenient way what orthodoxy would describe as the balanced nature of its own

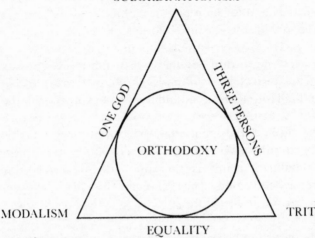

position. Moreover, it provides a ready explanation of the fact that often adversaries have confused orthodoxy with certain heretical positions. From the vantage point of a subordinationist, for instance, orthodoxy might be confused with modalism or with tritheism, because all three assert the full equality of the persons which subordinationism is concerned to deny. Thus Arius thought that Bishop Alexander of Alexandria was modalistic in his thought and expression. Arianism was in part a recoil against this putative danger. Similarly, a modalist may imagine that orthodoxy is either subordinationist or tritheistic. We are less concerned to trace out the misconceptions that tritheists may have, since they do not represent a significant movement within the Church.

It is important to recognise that the doctrine of the Trinity is a mystery. It is not, however, an absurdity, as some people have viewed it. Specifically, it is not asserted that God is one in the same respect in which he is three. What is propounded is that there is unity of essence, that this one essence is shared alike by each of the three persons, and that the three are conjoined in a total harmony of will and being, which far surpasses the unity observed between distinct individuals in humanity.[1]

In order to illustrate this truth, Christians of all ages have multiplied their efforts. Quite often, however, illustrations that have been offered are so far off the mark that they are injurious rather than helpful. For instance, it has been at times suggested that the three forms of water as ice, liquid, and vapour are representative of the Trinity. Indeed here we have a common chemical substance which, depending upon the temperature, takes varying physical forms. But this is illustrative of modalism more than it would be of the orthodox doctrine of the Trinity. Nothing here shows the interaction of the three in one. Under the circumstances it would seem that this illustration should be avoided because it may foster a wrong model. For the same reason the similes of the source, the rivulet, and the river, or the sun, the ray and the light, advanced by Tertullian (*Against Praxeas* 8), are to be adjudged very inadequate. Probably nothing that does not reflect some area of personality can be viewed as really appropriate.

Augustine in his great work *On the Trinity* has particularly explored the analogies between the Trinity and certain aspects of human psychological life. For instance, he analyses how love implies one person who loves, one other person who is loved, and love itself which binds these two. Similar analogies are found in the processes of knowledge and of consciousness. This approach may be seen as valid as indicative of a certain mutuality in God, but as a mirror of the divine trinitarian nature it limps, since it involves two persons plus an abstract notion, rather than three persons, as would seem to be required for an adequate analogy.

In *The Secret of the Universe*, Nathan R. Wood has explored in a most stimulating manner the question of the impact of the Trinity upon the structure of the world that the triune God has created. We cannot attempt here to give even a summary of the ideas contained in this book. Among the more meaningful parallels that Wood develops, one might mention three-dimensional space with its length, breadth, and height, or again time with its threefold components of future, present, and past. Here again personality is not a factor and therefore the illustration is wanting at a critical point; and yet the care with which the analogies are developed makes Wood's book especially arresting.[2]

In his work on the Trinity,[3] de Margerie has focused attention particularly upon the family as a reflection of the trinitarian nature of God. The advantage of an analogy which involves personality is obvious, but then the element of threeness does not appear indispensable, since a childless married couple do constitute a family and since many families include more than three members. Probably it is wise to recognise that certain aspects of the Trinity may be reflected in a limited way in the created world, but that nothing reflects it in its entirety, precisely because it is the prerogative of God alone to be triune, and he shares with nothing else this particular distinctive.[4]

II. IMPACT

The impact of the doctrine of the Trinity on the christian faith is very far reaching, for this doctrine fundamentally affects our understanding of God and of his relation to the world, particularly in terms of the redemptive purpose.

The doctrine of God is deeply affected by a trinitarian outlook since it represents God as possessing a sense of mutuality within his own being. The doctrine of the Trinity fosters an outlook upon God which emphasises life and movement within the Godhead. Without the trinitarian conception one could perhaps be embarrassed by the question 'What was God doing before he created the world?', for at this point the picture that would flash upon the screen would be that of a solitary being folded back upon himself and without opportunity for expressing in a meaningful way his life and perfections. God would then need the world in order to achieve self-expression and the independence of God would appear jeopardised. Of course, it might be thought that the question by its very nature transcends the power of our intellect and that we ought to be prepared therefore not to receive an answer that appears satisfactory to our minds. 'Here we have reached the limits', we might say, 'and any attempt to proceed beyond this is doomed to failure from the start!' There may be some truth to the observation, and we do not presume here to assert that we are offering a full answer to the query. Yet the doctrine of the Trinity helps us to apprehend in God something of his own inner life, and to see in him the intimate attachment of the Father to the Son, of the Son to the Father, of both of them to the Holy Spirit, and of the Holy Spirit to both of them. This may help us to grasp how God is self-sufficient and how creation, involving as it does all three persons of the Trinity, was not, however, necessary for God's own existence or happiness.

When we discuss the activities of God, especially his redemptive activity, we may perhaps discern even more closely the paramount significance of the Trinity. It is especially important to confess that the one who offered himself as a ransom for many is no other than God himself, so that the price of our redemption has actually been paid by the Son's infinite offering of himself on the cross of Calvary. This is therefore not a third party who benevolently assumes by divine appointment the crushing burden that we cannot bear, and who is commissioned by the Father to do this in order that the indebtedness of men might be settled before his judicial throne. Rather, in light of the doctrine of the Trinity we must see that in the person of Jesus Christ, God himself was incarnated, endured the full burden of our penalty and is therefore the proper basis for the redemption of anyone who is subsumed under him. The redemptive task was not accomplished by a third party entering the fray between the Father and the sinner, but it was the marvellous expression of the love and grace of the triune God, who in spite of the inexcusable character of man's offence was gracious enough to provide a plan for salvation, to effect himself all that was necessary for the fulfilment of that plan (work of Christ) and to apply himself to the sinner the benefits which were secured by his own work as the incarnate Mediator (work of the Holy Spirit). In representing the Holy Spirit as the one who does regenerate, sanctify, seal, and glorify the redeemed, the Scripture continues to show that it is God himself who is at work in the redemptive process.

Alternative views, in which man is seen as not in need of any objective help to be brought back to God, or in which the help that man receives is conceived as proferred by someone else than God himself, are deeply unsatisfactory. They make a representation of God which must be rated very heinous, since he appears in the guise of a celestial Shylock who insists on reparations and accepts them from someone else. Or else they represent God as very lax and unwilling, or unable, to enforce his laws, so that one can apparently violate them without being at all punished. It is the doctrine of the Trinity which places this subject in the proper perspective. In Jesus Christ, the God-man, the love of the Father, the love of the Son, and the love of the Holy Spirit, as well as the justice of the Father, the justice of the Son, and the justice of the Holy Spirit are operative and manifested. To separate them here is to work incredible havoc in the redemptive purpose. And yet, it is here that most clearly within Scripture they appear as distinct. This may well be the reason why the Trinity was only faintly adumbrated in the Old Testament revelation and did find its supreme and definitive expression in the New Testament, after the incarnation and exaltation of the great Mediator, Jesus Christ, the God-man. Truly there is more at stake here than a mere vowel.[5] The whole structure of the redemptive plan is inextricably connected with the truth of the Trinity.[6]

Gordon Conwell Theological Seminary   Roger Nicole
South Hamilton
Massachusetts

NOTES

1. The Trinity is presented as the supreme pattern for the unity of redeemed persons in the Church of God (John 17.11, 22f.; cf. Eph. 4.3–6).
2. Nathan R. Wood, *The Secret of the Universe* (Fleming H. Revell, New York, 1932).
3. Bertrand de Margerie, *La Trinité Chrétienne dans l'Histoire* (Beauchesne, Paris, 1975), Bibliography pp. 5–9.
4. A rather extensive discussion of the analogies of the Trinity, with an amazingly ample listing of suggestions proffered, may be found in H. Bavinck, *The Doctrine of God* (Eerdmans, Grand Rapids, 1951), pp. 321–30. (The original Dutch text, *Gereformeerde Dogmatiek*, 2nd ed. Kampen, Kok, 1908, II, 332–41, has many references which are omitted in the translation.)
5. The fact that just one *iota* differentiated the words *homo-ousios* (of the same essence) and *homoi-ousios* (of similar essence) in the controversies of the fourth century led Edward Gibbon to sneer that the orthodox who were ready to die for the truth of Christ's deity were martyrs for a vowel's sake.
6. The following works, in addition to those referred to above, may be found useful in studying the doctrine of the Trinity: Francis J. Hall, *The*

The Meaning of the Trinity

Trinity (Longmans, Green, New York, 1910, xx) (*Dogmatic Theology* IV);
Pohle-Preuss, *The Divine Trinity* (Herder, St Louis, 1946, iv) (*Dogmatic
Theology* II); Claude Welch, *In This Name: The Doctrine of the Trinity in
Contemporary Theology* (Charles Scribner's Sons, New York, 1952).

CHAPTER TWO

The New Testament

My purpose is limited in that I shall discuss only the degree to which there are elements of a doctrine of the Trinity in the New Testament and to what extent the New Testament writers were conscious of the doctrine of the Trinity as an issue.

I. THE ELEMENTS OF THE QUESTION

In the most general terms the elements of the doctrine of the Trinity are the threefoldness of God as Father, Son and Spirit, and, at the same time, the unity of God as one Being. In the case of the New Testament these elements resolve themselves into three questions. First of all, how far the writers take over the belief of the Old Testament in one God; that is, to what extent there is continuity and/or discontinuity with the view of God in the Old Testament? Secondly, there is the question of the position of Christ; how far is he already seen as divine and how is that related to the view of God in the Old Testament? And, thirdly, there is the question of the place of the Holy Spirit in the new covenant in contrast to the old covenant.

1. Continuity with the doctrine of the one God of the Old Testament – and discontinuity.
Throughout the whole history of christian theology it has been continuously emphasised that Jesus did not bring a

novel or radically different relevation of God from that which
had been revealed in the Old Testament. In the early Church
the Old Testament was taken over as a christian book by
most christian writers.[1] Within the New Testament it is clear
that Jesus himself saw his mission and his own life and death
as in continuous line with the revelation of God in the Old
Testament. His mission and achievement were a part of and
a fulfilment of the history of Israel.[2] He calls people back to
the law when they ask him about eternal life, as for example
with the rich young man, and he is careful to instruct the
leper whom he has healed to do what Moses had commanded
(Mark 10.17–22; 1.44). He appeals to the law in his own
teaching and his rejection of the tradition of the elders is on
the grounds that it invalidates the law. He has come, he says
in the Sermon on the Mount, not to destroy the law and the
prophets but to fulfill them. According to John he declares
that Abraham rejoiced to see his day (John 8.56).

Yet, on the other hand, Jesus seems to scandalise his
contemporaries on points of his obedience to the law and the
tradition. Not only does this apply to the question of whether
one should do good or not on the sabbath but also to such
questions as whether or not Jesus' disciples are at fault in
plucking corn on the sabbath (Mark 2.23ff.). The criticism of
the failure of his disciples to observe the ritual ablutions
before meals in Mark 7 draws a stinging response from him.
He attacks the Pharisees as blind leaders and the lawyers as
hypocrites (Luke 11.45–52). Jesus is clearly out of step with
his contemporaries on certain points of obedience to the law
and the tradition which were regarded by his contemporaries
as being of considerable importance.

Not only so, but Jesus also places his own words in a
strikingly high position. He says that his words will last for
ever (Mark 13.31) and his presence and teaching bring
responsibility to his generation; his generation is unfavour-

ably compared with that in Sodom and Gomorrah (Matt. 10.15; 11.20–24). Indeed, men will be judged by his words (John 12.40–50), and his authority to forgive sins is provocatively related in Mark 2.1–10 with his power to heal.

These two themes – continuity with the Old Testament and its fulfilment by Jesus on the one hand; and on the other, discontinuity between Jesus' teaching and both the Old Testament and its interpretation by his contemporaries – may be illustrated from two passages in the Sermon on the Mount. In Matthew 5.17 Jesus says, 'Think not that I have come to abolish the law and the prophets; I have come not to abolish them but to fulfil them'. He then goes on to say that neither an iota nor a dot will pass away from the law until all is accomplished and that those who relax the least of the commandments shall be called least in the Kingdom of Heaven. Clearly Jesus is not setting himself over against the Old Testament, the law and the prophets. But he makes some sharp contrasts between what had been said to the men of old and what he himself says in the matter of murder, adultery, false swearing, retaliation and loving your neighbour. One might then compare the final two sayings in the sermon when having completed his teaching, Jesus says that the criterion for entry into the Kingdom of God is for those who say, 'Lord, Lord', to him to also do his works. He then goes on to tell a story comparing a man who hears Jesus' words and does them to a wise man who built his house on the rock. The foolish man who hears the words but does not do them is like someone who builds his house on the sand. The point is clear. Jesus' words are definitive for a knowledge of God and his will and his words must be obeyed.

Not only is there a combination of continuity and discontinuity in the teaching of Jesus and in his references to his fulfilment of the Old Testament but there are significant discontinuities of an institutional kind between the New

Testament position and that of the Old Testament. In the Old Testament the Temple, the Nation and the Land constitute important *foci* for the revelation of God to his people. The Temple is where God's presence with his people is to be found; the Nation is the nation of God's redeemed people; and the Land is the inheritance promised to the fathers and taken by the people of Israel because of God's promise to them. The early Christians, however, did not take over these institutions in this way at all.[3] In John 4 Jesus cleanses the temple in Jerusalem and then declares that he can raise the destroyed temple in three days. This saying is interpreted in the Gospel tradition as a reference to the replacement of the temple as the sign of the presence of God with his people by the risen Christ. In 2 Corinthians 6 Paul speaks of the christian group which meets in the name of Christ as a temple, an idea which is not unrelated to the saying in Matthew 18.20: 'Where two or three are gathered in my name there am I in the midst of them'. When Jesus comes to Jerusalem for his final confrontation with the Jewish authorities in Mark's Gospel the debates with the Jewish leaders in Mark 12 are introduced with the parable of the wicked husbandmen. That parable clearly indicated to the Jewish leaders in Jerusalem and to the christian tradition that the nation was to be taken away from the Jewish leaders. This same point is made in John 11.47 where the Jewish authorities debate what they are to do with Jesus for he performs many signs. 'If we let him go on thus, everyone will believe in him, and the Romans will come and destroy both our Holy place and our nation.' In John's ironic style this clearly is what the Christian Gospel tradition understands to have taken place. The place of the land as the inheritance promised to the fathers is now in the New Testament taken by the Christ himself and his brothers. Worship is not defined in terms of locality but in terms of character in John 4.

'In sum, for holiness of place, Christianity has fundamentally, though not consistently, substituted the holiness of person; it has Christified holy space.'[4]

Not only is there a radical reappraisal and rejection of the institutions of nation, temple and land in the New Testament but there are also changes in the sense and character of divine obligations. In a recent article Professor U. Luz has drawn attention to the significance of the ethical teaching of Jesus for an understanding of Jesus' doctrine of God.[5] Commencing with a consideration of Mark 7.15, Professor Luz concludes that the emphasis in Jesus is switched from the cultic to the moral law. The particular emphasis on the moral law is to be seen in the way in which the great commandment to love God and to love the neighbour are linked together by Jesus. Already in Judaism the love of God is thought of as being fundamentally seen in the love of the neighbour but in Jesus this gains a new emphasis. God is now present in the neighbour and that point requires the teaching of Jesus. More particularly he is present in the human being who is in need. This implies a radical democratisation of religion such that rich and poor may now fulfil the commandments to God. It also means a radical simplification and an extension of the possibility of faith to all men, Jew and Gentile alike. It implies the command of God cannot be evaded; God is present in the needy neighbour everywhere. This particular point is a distinct input into the Jewish tradition by Jesus.

The hidden God who appears in the present and in weakness, is the God of Jesus. The God who will manifest himself in the future, who will reveal himself in the future as the universal judge, is the God of the Jewish tradition. Jesus' preaching of God, is characterised by the fact that he lets the God of the Jewish tradition who is to become manifest in the future be present at the present time, though not in such a way that the future is anticipated thereby, but in such a way that God is present in weakness and paves the way for the as yet still invisible universal judge.[6]

There is thus a clear sense of continuity between the New Testament understanding of God and the obligations that men owe to him and that in the Old Testament. The New Testament is not speaking of a new God nor does it offer a radical restatement of the character of God so as to change fundamentally the Old Testament picture. However, Jesus does display a personal authority which is exercised in word and deed. There is also the recurring theme of Jesus revealing God in terms of suffering and service and of his calling others to share his own vocation in this respect. There is a note of 'presentness' and of universality in this revelation of God. Locality in relation to God has gone; there is a new locality, namely Jesus himself.

On the one hand Jesus' belief that he is fulfilling the Old Testament in some sense and on the other hand the presence of significant discontinuities between the emphasis which he gives as compared with that in the Old Testament raise an important question as to how he is actually interpreting the Old Testament. One may illustrate this from John 7.40–44 where attempts to explain who Jesus is in terms of an interpretation of the Scripture fail. There is division amongst the people and their methods of looking at the Old Testament with a view to identifying the expected Christ or the Prophet do not enable them to identify Jesus. Also one may note the difficulties that the disciples have in understanding how it is that Jesus is to suffer and to die, and how that is to be related to an understanding of him as the expected or promised Messiah. There is not only the question of an understanding of the Messiah involved here; there is also the question of how the Old Testament is being interpreted by Jesus.

2. *Christology*

The second major element in a discussion of the Trinity of the New Testament must of course be the question of Christology. However, this is such a very large subject that it is only possible to touch on a few points. I would like to do this by referring to the very interesting argument in the central section of *The Origin of Christology* by C. F. D. Moule.[7] He is concerned to show that development is a better model for the understanding of the emergence of christological formulations than evolution, and that Paul's understanding of Christ as personal but more than individual is of very considerable importance. He discusses the four main titles of Jesus: the Son of Man, Son of God, Christ and Lord. In general his conclusion here is that the meaning of the terms is dictated by what Jesus himself was rather than by extraneous factors entering the stream of tradition from elsewhere. However, it is chapter 2 on 'The Corporate Christ' which is of most interest to us here. Here Professor Moule is concentrating on Paul and he draws attention first of all to the incorporative phrases which Paul uses. He uses the phrase 'in' Christ more than any other New Testament writer. However, only a few of these instances actually require the idea of 'incorporation'. These references are Romans 8.1, 16.7; 1 Corinthians 15.22; 2 Corinthians 5.17 and Philippians 3.8f. The testimony of these verses is that Christ is the *locus* where believers are found. This teaching is not balanced by an equivalent emphasis on Christ's indwelling of believers. There are a few close phrases in Paul's letters, as for example in Galatians 4.19, 'Until Christ be formed in you', but it is only in Ephesians 3.17 that a complete phrase is found, 'That Christ may dwell in your hearts through faith'.

On the contrary the indwelling agent for Paul is the Spirit. This pattern in Paul is in contrast with the Johannine which is quite reciprocal, as for example in John 17.21, 'Even as thou Father, art in me, and I in thee, that they also may be in us, so that the world may believe that thou hast sent me'. Such reciprocity is more compatible with relations between individuals. Professor Moule then considers the two images of Body and Temple. The Body is the more important of these images and in several parts at least of the Pauline epistles reflects an experience of Christ as a 'corporate person', to be joined to whom is to become a part of an organic whole. This is enormously significant when it is a theist who is speaking. The Temple is not as significant an image for Paul, according to Professor Moule, and this may be due to the fact that Jesus was a person who had died and been raised and that therefore the image of Body was more powerful and more able to be related to him as a known person. Professor Moule's fundamental conclusion, cast into the context of Paul as a theist, is very important for identifying an early 'high christology'.

Paul does seem to conceive of the living Christ as more than individual, while still knowing him vividly and distinctly as fully personal. He speaks of Christian life as lived in an area which is Christ; he speaks of Christians as incorporated in him. He thinks of the Christian community as (ideally) a harmoniously co-ordinated living organism like a body, and, on occasion, thinks of Christ as himself the living body of which Christians are limbs. All this is very puzzling; but one thing seems to emerge clearly from it: Paul, at least, had religious experiences in which the Jesus of Nazareth who had recently been crucified – this same person, without a shadow of doubt as to his identity – was found to be more than individual. He was found to be an 'inclusive' personality and this means, in effect, that Paul was led to conceive of Christ as any theist conceives of God: personal, indeed, but transcending the individual category.[8]

This discussion of Paul together with the study of the titles of Jesus earlier in the book provides a most significant argument for the early emergence of a very high christology. Indeed there is the suggestion here that Jesus was from the beginning Lord, even in some sense God. The model of development that is here being defended implies that the later christology of some sections of the New Testament are developments from what was there in the beginning. This means that in some sense later christology in the New Testament can be traced back to Jesus himself. What Jesus therefore did, said, and was is of crucial and decisive significance for christology in the New Testament period. This argument has a great deal of interest in its own right, but it has an interest in another respect as well. If, when we come to the question of how we might appropriately use the New Testament in discussions of christology or the Trinity, the function of the New Testament as historical witness to the Jesus who was there in the beginning, namely the historical Jesus, will be of very considerable importance, if Professor Moule's argument is correct. His argument carries with it the implication that the use of the New Testament as historical witness to the actual person who is the subject of christological formulations is of considerable importance.

3. Holy Spirit

The early Christians generally speak of a Christian as being in some sense in relationship with Christ. They also, however, speak of a Christian as being in relationship with the Spirit. In Paul becoming a Christian means receiving the

Spirit. For example, in Romans 5.5 he says that the love of God is poured into our hearts through the Holy Spirit which has been given to us. The Spirit it often conjoined with the terminology of power (*dunamis*) and is also related in 1 Corinthians to the working and division of gifts in the congregation, though in Romans and Ephesians this connection between gifts and Spirit is not made. The experience of the Spirit by the Christian is often related by Paul to the future hope and expectation of the Christian. This is especially true in Romans 8 where, in a discussion of 'adoption' and 'inheritance', it is the Spirit who enables the Christian to cry 'Abba, Father' and sustains him in his hope of his inheritance.

In comparison with the Old Testament Paul's statements on the Spirit are not all that remarkable. They suggest two modifications. First, that the Spirit now is thought of in more personal and continuing terms in the experience of all believers instead of being the power which comes upon some to enable them to do some unusual task. This contrast is not, of course, absolute. It is also the case that Paul's statements about the Spirit have a moral significance which is drawn out much more decisively than is the case in the Old Testament. Secondly, the Spirit for Paul points to the future resurrection. This is undoubtedly a significant modification of the Old Testament and like the first is to be attributed to his general theological readjustment from Judaism to take account of the resurrection of Jesus and of the expectation of a resurrection for those who belong to Jesus.

It is in Luke, however, that there is a strong historical sense of the significance of the coming of the Spirit. In the Acts of the Apostles Pentecost marks the commencement of the age of the Spirit. Here the Spirit is outpoured in fulfilment of the prophecies of Joel and Isaiah about the last days.[9] This also is a decisive form of realised eschatology. The outpouring of the Spirit promised for the last days now takes place in the present. This does not, of course, eliminate the more personal ways of speaking about the Spirit, but it does provide a framework in history which the more personal statements of Paul do not.

II. THE OVERALL ISSUE OF THE TRINITY

Here I wish to consider how far trinitarianism is a conscious issue for the New Testament writers. That is to say, how far are the elements of Father, Son and Spirit consciously seen and discussed in relation to the unity of God. It is not easy to decide when something is a conscious issue for the documents themselves are mostly occasional in character. Further it may be that questions of a trinitarian kind were not the subject treated in these documents simply because they were written to answer different questions.

There are a number of threefold formulae of a confessional or credal kind in the New Testament and these reveal the author's background, and also the sort of material which he could quote and anticipate being understood by his readers.[10] Then, secondly, there are occasions where the triad of Father, Son and Spirit appear in some emphatic way but no attempt is made to explain the precise relationship between them. So, for example, in the synoptics, Jesus' baptism, especially in Matthew's account, shows Father, Son and Spirit present. This is also true of Luke 1.35, 'The Holy Spirit will come upon you, the power of the most high will overshadow you; therefore the child to be born will be called Holy, the Son of God'.

Arthur Wainwright has suggested that the problem of unity and threefoldness is appreciated in the New Testament, and an explanation attempted pre-eminently by John but also to a lesser extent by Paul.[11] His argument in relation to Paul is based on the structure of the argument in Romans,

Corinthians and Galatians which he claims is trinitarian in form, and the argument in relation to John is on the basis of the Father-Son material and the Paraclete sayings (compare John 14.26 and John 20.21f.).

It is certainly true that the Lucan writings may be construed in trinitarian terms as providing a basis for a style of economic trinity. That is, there is a time of the Spirit which followed the time of the Son (Jesus' death and resurrection) and which itself was the fulfilment of the revelation of God through Israel and the prophets. However, this way of construing an economic Trinity not only has difficulties in itself[12] but in the Lucan writings it is not really possible to represent this division as a concern for trinitarian questions. Rather, the life, death and resurrection of Jesus is seen by Luke as part of the fulfilment of the purposes of God in the history of Israel and anticipated by the prophets. The coming of the Spirit at Pentecost is a bringing into the present of eschatological events portrayed in the prophets. The springs of the Lucan 'economy' are prophecy, history and fulfilment rather than concerns about a trinitarian concept of God.

In the Johannine material it is perfectly true that the question of the relation between the Father and the Son is dwelt on at some length, as is also the question of the relationship between the Spirit and the Son and thus, also, to a lesser extent the relationship between the Father and the Spirit. However, once again, concerns that are being expressed in this literature are not trinitarian concerns. Rather they are concerns related to the position of the post resurrection convert. How do those who become Christians after the time of Jesus know Jesus and thus know also the Father? We do not yet have a discussion of this matter as related to the threefoldness and unity of God.

Thus it appears that in the New Testament there are clear

elements for a doctrine of the Trinity. There is a commitment to the unity of God as in the Old Testament, albeit with some modifications of the way in which God is thought to have been revealed; there is a development of a considerable christological tradition and there are some important suggestions of an understanding of the Holy Spirit as revealing the presence of God. However we do not have in precise terms a conscious discussion of the doctrine of the Trinity as an issue.

III. THE DOCTRINE OF THE TRINITY AND THE NEW TESTAMENT

If it is the case that in the New Testament we do not have a conscious discussion of the doctrine of the Trinity in even the most elementary form, but have simply what might be called elements for a doctrine of the Trinity, then certain questions must be raised as to how one might appropriately use the New Testament, and indeed the Old Testament as well, in any discussion of the doctrine of the Trinity. Professor Wiles has suggested that in the early Church thought about God developed because of the need to refute heresy, the need to defend and explain the Faith and also because Christian people wanted to understand more fully their own christian faith. He also argues that doctrinal arguments were influenced by two very large prior factors: prayer, or christian piety in relation to Jesus, and soteriology, the principle that Jesus saves and saves effectively. Scripture, he suggests, in this context, has an indirect role.[13] For example, the use by Arius of Psalm 110.3, 'I begat thee before the morning star', illustrates how the role of Scripture 'was rather confirmatory of a position originally adopted for quite other reasons'. Of course, by the time of the Arian debates the status and character of the New Testament documents had gone through considerable developments since the first century.

While the analysis of the emergence of patristic doctrine as outlined by Professor Wiles may be the subject for debate amongst patristic scholars the issue which is raised by him is of continuing significance. If the doctrine of the Trinity is to be taken as being central to contemporary Christianity then the way in which the New Testament is used in any formulation of a doctrine of the Trinity needs to be considered with some care. It cannot be simply taken as the foundation upon which a superstructure is built. It is not at all clear what might be meant by a foundation in this context, as Karl Barth pre-eminently has demonstrated.[14]

It seems to me that there are at least three points of importance which might be drawn from the above discussion. First, there is the question of how a doctrine of the Trinity might be related to a commitment to the authority of the New Testament in doctrinal discussion and formulation. If it is the case that there is no doctrine of the Trinity as such in the New Testament, and yet one wants to hold to a doctrine of the Trinity in some form, then there clearly must be a place for some kind of acceptable and proper doctrinal development. Because we are dealing here with the question of development immediately from the New Testament period, and indeed within the New Testament itself, we are faced with a consideration of development which questions the very nature of the New Testament documents as 'Scripture'.[15]

Secondly, Jesus' commitment to the idea that he was fulfilling the hopes of Israel, while at the same time revealing something new and different, raises the question of how the Old Testament is to be interpreted. The presence of a commitment to some sense of continuity with manifest discontinuity requires not just a simple statement that there is continuity and discontinuity but it demands such a formulation of the idea of fulfilment that discontinuities can be reasonably explained. The evidence of the New Testament suggests that Jesus was in some sense an innovator in the eyes of his contemporaries in the way in which he interpreted the Old Testament. The fact that he may have used similar exegetical methods to some of his Jewish contemporaries does not mean that his fundamental hermeneutical approach was the same as theirs, nor indeed necessarily similar to theirs.

Thirdly, the argument I have outlined above in regard to Jesus' own authority, and his person in relation to christology, raises immediately the question of how far the New Testament ought to be regarded in christological discussion as evidence for the historical Jesus. This may not exhaust, of course, the ways in which a theologian might like to use the New Testament, but if the argument is sound then this usage may not properly be excluded.[16]

St John's College,   BRUCE N. KAYE
Durham

[*Editors' note.* Dr Kaye recognises that some scholars and other contributors do take the view that a concern of certain biblical writers was a genuine trinitarian concern. This view is well presented by Arthur W. Wainwright, *The Trinity in the New Testament* (London, 1969).]

NOTES

1. See H. von Campenhausen, *The Formation of the Christian Bible* (London, 1972); P. R. Ackroyd and C. F. Evans (eds.) *The Cambridge History of the Bible*, 1 (Cambridge, 1970); A. Sundberg, *The Old Testament of the Early Church* (Cambridge, Mass., 1964).
2. O. Cullmann, *Salvation in History* (London, 1967); J. Jeremias, *New Testament Theology*, 1 (London, 1971), pp. 42ff.; G. A. G. Knight, *A Biblical Approach to the Doctrine of the Trinity* (Edinburgh/London, 1953).

3. See B. N. Kaye, *Using the Bible in Ethics* (Bramcote, 1976).
4. W. D. Davies, *The Gospel and the Land* (Berkeley/Los Angeles/London, 1974), p. 368.
5. U. Luz, 'On the Interpretation of God given by Jesus' *Universitas* 15, 1973, pp. 169–78.
6. Ibid., p. 175.
7. *The Origin of Christology* (Cambridge, 1977). See also M. Hengel, *The Son of God* (London, 1976) and the different approach of P. Gerlitz, *Ausserchristliche Einflüsse auf die Entwicklung des Christlichen Trinitäts-dogmas* (Leiden, 1963). See also F. Hahn, *The Titles of Jesus in Christology* (London, 1969).
8. op. cit., p. 95. Cf. T. W. Manson, *The Teaching of Jesus* (Cambridge, 1931), p. 236.
9. Acts 2.14–36. See J. D. G. Dunn, *Baptism in the Holy Spirit* (London, 1970), ch. 4.
10. e.g. Matt. 28.19; 1 Cor. 12.4–6; 2 Cor. 13.14. For further examples and discussions see O. Cullmann, *The Earliest Christian Confessions* (London, 1949); J. N. D. Kelly, *Early Christian Creeds* (London, 1950); and A. W. Wainwright, *The Trinity in the New Testament* (London, 1962), pp. 237ff.
11. op. cit., pp. 248ff.
12. See M. Wiles 'Some Reflections on the Origins of the Doctrine of the Trinity', *J.T.S.* n.s. 8 (1957), pp. 92–106, reprinted in M. Wiles, *Working Papers in Doctrine* (London, 1976), pp. 1–17; and C. Welch, *The Trinity in Contemporary Theology* (London, 1953), pp. 239ff.
13. M. Wiles, *The Making of Christian Doctrine* (Cambridge, 1967); see also H. E. W. Turner, *The Pattern of Christian Truth* (London, 1954); J. Pelikan, *The Christian Tradition*, i, *The Emergence of the Catholic Tradition (100–600)* (Chicago/London, 1971); J. Lebreton, *History of the Dogma of the Trinity* (London, 1939) and G. Kretschmar, *Studien zur frūchristlichen Trinitätstheologie* (Tübingen, 1956).
14. K. Barth, *Church Dogmatics*, i.i (Edinburgh, 1936). See also E. Jüngel, *The Doctrine of the Trinity. God's Being is in Becoming* (Edinburgh, 1976), especially ch. 1.
15. See further P. Toon, *The Development of Doctrine in the Church* (Grand Rapids, 1979).
16. For a recent analysis see D. H. Kelsey, *The Uses of Scripture in Recent Theology* (London, 1975). One might contrast here the remarks of Austin Farrer, *The Glass of Vision* (Westminster, 1948), pp. 132ff.; and see also J. L. Houlden, *Patterns of Faith* (London, 1977).

CHAPTER THREE

The Discernment of Triunity[1]

The theological literature has been greatly enriched in recent decades by detailed studies of the nature of religious 'discernment' or 'divination'. The works of Rudolf Otto, Mircea Eliade, and Ian Ramsey,[2] in particular, and from various perspectives, have contributed much to our understanding of characteristic situations in which men may intuit or apprehend the immediate presence of deity. This 'empirical-phenomenological' approach (to characterise it as broadly as possible) represents a significant departure from the more traditional 'proofs' of deity based on logical argument or citations of Scripture in that (a) it requires an empirical 'grounding' in concrete, historically conditioned situations, and (b) it necessarily leaves the question of truth value open to review and re-evaluation by its appeal to specific acts of personal intuition or discernment. Therefore, in comparison with the traditional 'proofs', there is a certain loss of cogency, but, on the other hand, a distinct gain in concreteness and accessibility to the religious imagination of the individual.

The empirical-phenomenological approach raises serious difficulties, however, for contemporary evaluations of the traditional doctrine of the Trinity. The phenomenological model of discernment has, for all its epistemological difficulties, a rather simple structure. It involves two basic terms: an empirical-secular event, and a numinous-sacred presence, which it relates in dipolar or dialectic fashion.[3] Hence, it is anchored in the empirical plane and points 'beyond' the empirical in a (figuratively) 'vertical' direction.[4] Such a 'disclosure' model may account for relatively simple Christian discernments like the apostolic recognition of God's presence in Jesus, but these discernments alone would most readily lead to a doctrine of simple 'adoption' or 'inspiration' as the early history of christian thought surely indicates. The difficulty is that the 'orthodox', patristic doctrine of 'triunity' is much richer and more complex than a simple dipolar relation between the secular and the sacred. 'Triunity' involves not only the 'vertical' dimension of disclosure or 'revelation', but several rather subtle 'intra-trinitarian' relations that transcend space and time and are, therefore, very difficult to discern from empirical grounds.

These considerations lead us to query whether there are any empirical, i.e. historically-verifiable, situations in the life of Jesus that could conceivably give rise to a specific discernment of 'triunity', as opposed to a simpler doctrine like 'adoptionism' or 'modalism', and, if so, whether the empirical-phenomenological model of discernment is sufficient to account for such a complex disclosure, or whether some additional considerations are also required. Of course, the mere existence of an appropriate setting in the life of Jesus would not necessarily imply that the disciples, or the evangelists, actually discerned triunity therein, or even that the gradual emergence of trinitarian speculation had its source therein. Questions of historical development are not of primary concern in the present investigation. The issue at hand is not how trinitarian thought actually developed, but whether it is 'meaningful' in terms of the empirical-phenomenological model of discernment. Historical considerations may be brought in for 'corroboration', as it were, but they are not decisive in questions of truth value, or even in questions of 'meaningfulness' which are prerequisite to the consideration of truth value.

The only way to answer the question posed above is to sift through all the material in the gospel narratives looking for possible situations meeting the required conditions. Fortunately, we can specify the kind of situation we are looking for in advance and work toward the New Testament material quasi-deductively. For example, situations in which the 'deity' of Christ might be discerned (e.g. miraculous healings, prophetic teachings, acts of forgiveness), while *necessary* for the discernment of triunity, are not *sufficient* in themselves since they allow 'monarchian' interpretations as well as more 'orthodox' ones. So the kind of situation required must be such that more than one divine presence is 'revealed' at the same time. That is, there must be occasions in which a dual, or multiple, manifestation of some kind may be taken to reflect a dual or multiple structure in the Godhead.

This stipulation immediately brings to mind the kinds of situations in which God is discerned to have said, 'This is my Son . . .', i.e. the baptism and transfiguration of Jesus (Mark 1.11, 9.7). However, the proto-trinitarian form of these incidents makes it extremely difficult for us to determine their empirical content. The 'Father-Son' relation may have already been intuited on other grounds by the time the baptism and transfiguration traditions assumed their present form. Hence these incidents seem more like symbolic representations of a 'known' feature of the Godhead than occasions for the discernment of an unknown one. But even aside from the problems of historical criticism, the very uniqueness of these situations renders them insufficient for the discernment of ontological triunity. The occurrence of a few disclosures of the 'This is my Son' variety would not in itself provide adequate grounds for the unarbitrary discernment of two divine 'persons' since one might equally well intuit the presence of a single 'person' in alternative manifestations or modalities. Any appeal to other highlights of the gospel narrative, such as the cross or resurrection, must be regarded as inadequate, in terms of the present investigation, for similar reasons.

In other words, no set of isolated incidents in the life of Jesus can provide the grounds required for the meaningful discernment of a plurality of persons in the Godhead. What is required, therefore, is not an event or series of events, but an empirical setting or condition which characterises the life of Jesus as a whole. That is, there must be some characteristic feature in the life of Jesus that allows repeatable, or even continual discernment of the presence of God in two or more persons and is not confined to the revelatory highlights of the narrative. The dialogue of 'Father' and 'Son', which may have been intuited at the baptism and transfiguration, must be seen to be a general condition of Jesus' everyday life.

When the problem is reformulated in this way, we are immediately led to a consideration of the prayer life of Jesus as observed by the disciples.[5] In the everyday prayers of Jesus, some of which are reflected in the Gospels, we have a possible empirical situation which satisfies the three necessary conditions: (a) it is relatively accessible to historical investigation, (b) it characterises Jesus' life as a whole, from baptism right through to the cross,[6] and (c) it involves a dialogue between Jesus and his 'Father' which could conceivably give rise to the discernment of (at least) two divine 'persons'.

Having arrived at a possible situation for the discernment of triunity, let us turn the problem around, i.e. start with what we may reasonably affirm concerning the prayers of Jesus in the context of his life as a whole (relying here on Jeremias), and ask what conditions must be satisfied in order to allow a meaningful discernment of triunity. First, then, there is Jesus himself and the distinctive quality of his life. We must suppose that God is discerned to be present in Jesus, not only in miraculous deeds and prophetic words, but as a continual, normal condition of his life. In his eating, in his sleeping, in all the everyday events of life he must be seen to be God in the flesh, literally God incarnate. Presumably this is a matter of historical discernment on the part of the disciples even though it may represent a post-resurrection 'recollection'. Aside from the possible retrospective element, however, the discernment itself can readily be understood on the basis of the phenomenological model we are using provided that it allows for the recognition of ontological 'qualities' and not just a bare, numinous 'presence'. The presence of God in Jesus was, in fact, discerned to be a continual, irrevocable presence ('God with us', the 'Word made flesh'), not just an occasional one as in the Old Testament theophanies. Moreover, it was not a mere 'dynamic' presence, or a mediated one as in the prophets and miracle workers, but an immediate, 'personal' presence of God as reflected in the dramatic incidents of the revision of the law, healing on the Sabbath, and the forgiving of sins. In all, then, there are three essential elements of discernment here: (1) the simple presence of God in Jesus, (2) the continual, irrevocable nature of this presence, which is required, as we shall see, to rule out or discern against modalistic alternations, and (3) the immediate, 'personal' quality of this presence, which is required to account for insistence on the full deity of the 'Son' and later discernments against the claims of 'subordinationism' and Arianism.

Then, secondly, Jesus was known to pray to the Father daily (Luke 9.18), and, presumably, the Father was always present to hear and respond to these prayers (John 11.41f.). On occasions, the Father is believed to have responded audibly (Luke 3.21f., 9.28–36, John 12.27ff.). Perhaps the 'voice' of the Father was discerned by the disciples in some suitably numinous empirical phenomenon like 'thunder' (cf. John 12.29). Be that as it may, we have in situations like these a double-discernment on the part of the disciples: God is in the 'thunder' (a familiar Old Testament manifestation); but, at the same time, God is also present in Jesus (in accordance with our previous considerations). Moreover, while audible responses of the Father may only have been discerned in isolated instances like the baptismal and transfigurational declarations, the situation involved in these prayers was characteristic of Jesus' life as a whole in a way that baptism and transfiguration were not. In fact, the *continual* presence of the Father, in dialogue with Jesus, could readily have been discerned even when there was no audible response at all. Jesus prays to the Father: it is evidently to God that he prays; but he that is praying is also discerned to be God (incarnate). In the prayer life of Jesus, then, we have an empirical situation that characterises Jesus' life as a whole and at the same time allows the repeatable, or even continual, discernment of God in two 'persons'.[7]

Of course, even a continual double-discernment would not prove that there really are two divine persons. God is also believed to be omnipotent and omnipresent. Certainly he could engineer a continual dual-manifestation like this, even if he had only one 'person' to man the job and was not allowed to 'alternate' between manifestations due to the continuity of his presence in Jesus. None the less, the un-ambiguous appearance of duality is there and is character-istic of the prayer life of Jesus. Hence, the discernment of two divine persons is, at least, meaningful. Moreover, it could readily be 'legitimised' by an appeal to the 'faithfulness' of God, or, in hermeneutical terms, by an appeal to the theo-logical principle that God is in himself what he is (or appears to be) in his revelation.[8] The situation is complex, but, at least it is consistent with the terms of the phenomenological model of discernment.

In spite of all these stipulations, we have still not arrived at anything like a doctrine of 'triunity', or even 'biunity'. The discernment of two divine persons, by itself, would probably lead us to 'bitheism', the belief in two separate, but equal, 'gods'. So we must appeal to some additional characteristic of Jesus' prayer life such as the disturbing intimacy of Jesus' relation with the Father as reflected in his unusual use of the term 'Abba'. Jeremias's research on the prayers of Jesus may not have settled all disputes as to the uniqueness of Jesus' use of this term, but it does serve to point out the unusual quality of 'mutuality' or 'reciprocity' between Jesus and the Father and highlights its importance for New Testament theology.[9] There are verifiable, or at least researchable, grounds, then, for the discernment of an ontological relation of 'reciprocity' between the two divine persons, Father and Son, the existence and distinctness of which have already been discerned. At some stage of the tradition, the early Church must have recognised that the empirical dialogue between Jesus and his Father reflected an eternal, ontological relation of 'coinherence' between the two divine persons. Undoubtedly, the first clear recognition of this relationship may be attributed to the 'Johannine' tradition:[10] 'I in the Father, and the Father in me' (John 14.11, et passim).

It should be noted that the discernment of 'coinherence' would not be sufficient to account for the discernment of the Father-Son relationship if it were not for the accompanying recognition of the continual, immediate divine presence (of the 'Son') in Jesus himself. Coinherence, by itself, might be interpreted as a relation between a single divine person (the 'Father') and some subordinate, mediating aspect of the Godhead (e.g. the 'word', 'spirit', or 'glory' as conceived in the Old Testament), or even a single divine person and a creature (e.g. an angel or prophet). Together with the discernment of proper deity in Jesus, however, it leads to the notion of two coinhering, equally divine 'persons', i.e. two persons in one God, and hence to the concepts of a single 'substance' and an eternal 'generation'. In simpler, Johannine terminology: 'I and the Father are one' (John 10.30).

Thus far, we have concentrated on the problem of the first two persons of the Trinity, and success has not come easily, to say the least! Would it be going too far to suppose that the simple discernment model could be adapted to account for the recognition of the 'third' person? It seems that it would. The meaningful discernment of a distinct 'second' person, as we have seen, is only made possible by the empirical nature of the life of Jesus, or, in theological terms, by the 'Incarnation'. So we appear to be at a decided disadvantage with regard to the Holy Spirit who 'comes and goes' at will and refuses to anchor himself to the empirical world long enough for us to have a good look. The only instances in the New Testament where the Spirit is said to manifest himself directly (Jesus' baptism and Pentecost) are so momentary and ephemeral that modalistic interpretations could not be ruled out without danger of arbitrariness. In fact, the rough equivalence of 'Spirit' and 'Christ' in the Pauline corpus[11] might lead us to believe that the Spirit is simply another manifestation of the Son along the lines of Sabellianism. The baptismal formula in Matthew and the 'Spirit of the Son' motifs in Paul may have been sufficient evidence for Athanasius and the Cappadocian Fathers,[12] but, unfortunately for us, they are not susceptible to the empirical grounding required by the phenomenological model we have adopted.

If required to account for the recognition of a 'third' person in terms of empirically grounded acts of intuition, it seems that we must appeal to something like a 'discernment' of discernment. That is, we must not neglect the fact that, in addition to the prayers of Jesus and the responses of the Father, there is the apostolic discernment of the presence of God in both prayer and response which may have its own implications. By analogy with the Old Testament prophets, for instance, it might be concluded that the early Church could have apprehended the 'Word' of God in Jesus only through inspiration by the 'Spirit' of God. The very fact that the early Church could (retrospectively) apprehend the presence of God in Christ might be taken to imply that God was somehow present in the Church, as well.[13] In fact, there is ample evidence for such a belief in the New Testament itself (Rom. 8.14ff., Gal. 4.6f., 1 Cor. 12.3, 1 John 4.2f). This does not mean that the Church came to realise the presence of the Holy Spirit in the way I have described, only that the realisation was empirically grounded and phenomeno-logically meaningful, however it may have originated.

Not only did the early Church recognise the indwelling presence of the 'Spirit', but it experienced this presence to be continual and immediate like the presence of God appre-hended in Jesus, thus providing sufficient grounds for subsequent discernments that ruled out modalism and subordinationism (John 14.16f., Rom. 8.9ff., 1 Cor. 3.16, 12.12f.). Moreover, this immediate, continual divine presence in the Church was co-ordinated with the retro-spective apprehension of the immediate, continual presence of the 'Son' in Jesus and of the 'Father' responding to his prayers. All in all, then, this amounts to a threefold mani-festation of God: a dual manifestation in prayer and response (seen retrospectively) and a conjugate, third manifestation in the discerning Church itself, and it provides sufficient empirical grounds for the meaningful discernment of 'triunity'. At least, the apostolic association of the presence of

35

the Spirit with the apprehension of God as 'Father' (Rom. 8.15, Gal. 4.6) and Jesus as 'Lord' (1 Cor, 12.3) provided sufficient grounds for later theologians to infer the full equality and 'coinherence' of the three divine 'persons'. Moreover, the fact that the presence of the Spirit was experienced by the Church rather than discerned in an external manifestation (as the presence of Father and Son were) makes it unnecessary to postulate a 'fourth' person in order to account for the discernment of the first three. The subsequent limitation of the Godhead to three persons, then, is also meaningful in terms of the empirical context of the prayer life of Jesus and its evaluation by the early Church.

Since the apprehension of the Spirit within the Church is rather more subtle than the apprehension of the Father and Son without (i.e. in the past events of Jesus' life), it is perhaps not surprising that speculation concerning the Spirit is rather less developed in the New Testament than speculation about the Son.[14] The Spirit is the least conspicuous, the most 'transparent' of the three divine persons precisely because he is 'manifest' in the knowing 'subject' rather than in the known 'object'. In fact, the New Testament nowhere seems clearly to affirm the full deity of the Spirit or properly to define his relation to the Father and Son. He 'proceeds from the Father' (John 15.26), yet he functions as the 'Spirit of the Son' (Gal. 4.6). In view of the 'transparency' of the Spirit within the Church, it would seem that attempts to define these relations more exactly might not be very meaningful. The history of controversy about the *filioque* clause in the Western version of the Nicene creed appears to confirm this conclusion.

To summarise the results of our investigation: I find that the prayer life of Jesus, as observed by the disciples and the early Church, is a suitable empirical basis for the apostolic discernment of triunity and that it is possible to analyse the rather complex nature of this discernment into the following elements (in spite of the fact that they are organically inter-related, they are logically distinct):

1) The presence of God discerned in Jesus (miracles, pro-phetic teachings, etc.).
2) This presence discerned to be continual and irrevocable (everyday life, suffering, death).
3) This presence discerned to be immediate and 'personal' (revision of law, healing on sabbath, forgiving of sins); together with (2) implies 'Incarnation', 'God with us'.
4) This presence discerned in continual conjunction with the distinct personal presence of God-the-Father (prayers of Jesus, 'responses' of the Father); implies two distinct divine 'persons'.
5) These two divine presences discerned to be reciprocally related, 'coinherent' (intimacy of prayer, Jesus' use of 'Abba'); implies two 'persons' in one God (John 14.11, 10.30).
6) Discernment of these divine presences discerned to be due to divine 'inspiration', presence of Holy Spirit in the Church itself (1 Cor. 12.3).
7) Presence of the Spirit discerned to be continual, immediate, and intimately related to apprehension of God as 'Father' and Jesus as his 'Son' (Rom. 8.15, Gal. 4.6); implies three, and only three, 'coinhering', divine persons, one God.

All of these elements may be regarded as variations on the theme of 'religious discernment' or 'divination' (Otto, Eliade, Ramsey, *et al.*), but we have in passing noted three significant 'variations' from the simple phenomenological model which seem to indicate the need for further modelling. First, our analysis calls for the discernment of specific qualities in the Godhead, such as 'continuity', 'personality' and 'reciprocity', which go well beyond the simple discernment of the 'numinous'. Hence, we require some non-phenomenological principle like the belief that God is not deceptive in his acts of revelation, or that he is in himself what he is towards us in his revelation. Secondly, in order to account for the discernment of the 'third' person of the Trinity, it is necessary to allow for the recognition of the otherwise 'transparent' presence of divinity within the knowing 'subject' (the Church) as a reflex of the discernment of divinity in the known 'object' (Jesus). In phenomenological terms, this amounts to an appeal to the experience of 'inspiration' or 'enthusiasm'; in theological language, it leads to a doctrine of 'prevenient grace' or 'union with Christ' through the Holy Spirit. Finally, we find it necessary to allow for the discernment of unforeseen qualities in past events, as though they were actually present, since the bulk of the apostolic discernment concerning the life of Jesus probably took place after the Resurrection and Pentecost. Hence, we must appeal to some principle by which past events may be 'reviewed' and re-evaluated in the light of subsequent developments. Compare Cullmann's investigation of the reinterpretation of biblical tradition in the light of new developments in 'salvation history'[15] and Pannenberg's treatment of the 'retroactive effect' of the Resurrection on the significance of Jesus' life and teachings.[16] In short, the fundamentally an-historical approach of phenomenology must be supplemented by some consideration of 'tradition history'. In graphic terms, the 'vertical' relation between sacred and secular (being) must be co-ordinated with the 'horizontal' dimension of historical becoming.[17]

If nothing else, this little exercise displays the richness and complexity of the 'orthodox' doctrine of triunity and perhaps helps to account for the wide variety of simpler, 'heretical', formulations. At least seven distinct elements of discernment and three supplementary principles are required before we arrive at the 'high' doctrine defended by the fourth-century Fathers, and every intermediate stage of the journey is provided with tempting resting places for the discernment-weary. It would seem only an accident of history that the majority of the Church actually made it all the way, even if it did take four centuries to get there. After all, wasn't the historical development of trinitarian thought largely a matter of gradual accretion in the significance of christo-logical titles and then a series of unnecessarily stubborn reactions to rather attractive alternatives? By the time we reach the fourth century, the discussion has become so formalised and metaphysical that there does not seem to be any real connexion with the empirical life of Jesus or even the apostolic discernment, such as it was.

It is true that most of the patristic defence of triunity assumes more than Jesus' contemporaries could ever have realised. Still there are recurrent themes in their writings which seem to originate from precisely those empirical settings that we have been considering. I am particularly impressed by the second and third chapters of Hilary's treatise, *On the Trinity*, written in the late 350s AD. In order to refute the Arians, Hilary argues that the names of 'Father' and 'Son' must be taken in their ontological sense inasmuch as they constitute the burden of the revealing work of Christ, viz. the revelation of God as a true 'Father' in relation to his true 'Son'. What intrigues me here is the fact that he takes the 'coinherence' formula of John 14.11 and the 'high-priestly prayer' of John 17 ('His prayer to God') as his principal texts in chapter three. Hilary's attention is clearly fixed on the intimate 'mutual enveloping' of Father and Son and the 'mutual exchange of glory' which John so strikingly portrayed. Granted that it is a long way from Hilary to John, and from John back to the prayer life of Jesus, may we not see a possible thread of continuity in all this? It is neither historically determinative nor logically cogent, but the connexion is there, and it can be followed and evaluated in our own attempts to discern the possible triunity of God:

> The work which the Lord came to do was not to enable you to recognise the omnipotence of God as Creator of all things, but to enable you to know him as the Father of that Son who addresses you.[18]

Western Theological Seminary   CHRISTOPHER B. KAISER
Holland
Michigan

NOTES

1. Originally published in the *Scottish Journal of Theology*, Vo. 28, pp. 449ff.
2. R. Otto, *The Idea of the Holy* (London, 2nd end. 1950); M. Eliade, *Patterns in Comparative Religion* (London, 1958); I. T. Ramsey, *Religious Language* (London, 1957).
3. R. Otto, op. cit., pp. 27f., 144, 170; M. Eliade, op. cit., pp. 13, 26, 29.
4. Cf. Peter Berger's 'Signals of transcendence'; *A Rumour of Angels* (London, 1970), p. 70.
5. See J. Jeremias, *The Prayers of Jesus* (London, 1967).
6. Ibid., pp. 57, 76f.
7. Cf. Tertullian's argument against modalism in *Against Praxeas*, 23.
8. Cf. K. Barth, *Church Dogmatics*, I.i. (Edinburgh, 1936), p. 439; and II.i (1957), pp. 227, 260. Note: this is not a 'Barthian' principle so much as a patristic one; see e.g. Hilary, *On the Trinity*, II.8; IV.14; V.17.
9. J. Jeremias, op. cit., pp. 47, 53f., 62, 78. See also his *New Testament Theology*, Part One (London, 1971), pp. 36f.. See further R. Hamerton-Kelly, *God the Father* (Philadelphia, 1979), pp. 71–81.
10. J. Jeremias, op. cit., pp. 32, 48.
11. See A. W. Wainwright, *The Trinity in the New Testament* (London, 1962), pp. 215ff.
12. Athanasius, *Letters to Serapion*, I.2; Basil, *On the Holy Spirit*, 43f., 49.

13. Cf. J. McIntyre, *The Shape of Christology* (London, 1966), pp. 149f.
14. A. W. Wainwright, op. cit., pp. 199–234.
15. O. Cullmann, *Salvation in History* (London, 1967), pp. 88ff.
16. W. Pannenberg, *Jesus – God and Man* (London, 1968), pp. 321ff., 362f.
17. The importance of the 'horizontal' historical dimension is stressed by Eliade in his sequel to *Patterns*: *The Myth of the Eternal Return* (London, 1955), pp. 104ff.
18. Hilary, *On the Trinity*, II.22; *Nicene and Post-Nicene Fathers*, Second Series, Vol. IX (Oxford, 1894), p. 68.

CHAPTER FOUR

The Patristic Dogma

Current debate about the Trinity has largely gravitated from a detailed analysis of the person and work of the Godhead to starker, more fundamental questions. Does the framework of classical trinitarianism hold good for today? Can it be called 'biblical', and if so, in what sense? Is it binding on a culture which has rejected the thought-forms of ancient philosophy?

Our difficulties are made worse by serious problems of definition. What exactly do we mean when we speak of patristic trinitarian dogma? Even more problematic, how are we to understand the concept of validity in this context? Do we mean that the dogma must be in conformity to scriptural teaching, that it must be internally consistent, that it must be relevant for the present day, or is it some combination of these? It may seem pedantic to retreat to definitions of basic vocabulary, but there can be no doubt that much modern discussion has suffered from a failure either to define its terms with sufficient precision, or to appreciate the true significance of the context in which the traditional framework was elaborated.

It seems fairly clear in fact that we are faced with two basic issues in our discussion of patristic trinitarian dogma. The first concerns the validity, or better, the appropriateness, of dogmatism as a means of expressing christian belief. The second, more specific, concerns the elaboration of a particular doctrine in a series of credal statements in the fourth and fifth centuries of the christian era. We cannot logically discuss the second of these until we have come to terms with the first, particularly as it is now not infrequently argued that it is the framework of dogmatism which is more to blame than the genius of the patristic writers, who did their very best, as is often admitted, with tools unsuited to their task.

I. DOGMATISM

It is of course well known that dogmatism, as a form of structured thought, did not spring up from within the judaeo-christian tradition. It was in Greece, among men of ideas, that logical analysis was developed in a systematic way, and it was from the philosophers of Hellenism that the early christian thinkers learned their technique of intellectual self-expression. It was as Christianity spread across and into the Graeco-Roman world that its dogmatic structure developed; neither Judaism, nor Jewish Christianity, nor even the Syriac tradition offers anything at all comparable to it.

It is beyond dispute that Christianity took on the dress of a particular, and fundamentally alien, culture in the course of its early development; equally, it cannot be denied that other courses may have been possible, and that had Christianity remained within a Semitic orbit, it might have evolved a religious understanding more akin to that of later Judaism, or perhaps Islam. What we are concerned to examine therefore is not whether the actual historical development of mainstream Christianity was inevitable, for surely it was not, but whether it represents the true development of the fundamental data of the Faith. Did the early Fathers, consciously or not, twist the primitive revelation out of its context and meaning, or did they perceive and follow lines of evolution inherent in the original deposit?

This question has been hotly debated at least since the days of Harnack, whose thesis that dogmatism was Hellenism corrupting Christianity is still widely believed in outline, however much it may have been altered since in details. Two recent works which bring the matter back into the limelight are James Dunn's *Unity and Diversity in the New Testament* (London, 1977) and Bernard Lonergan's *The Way to Nicea* (London, 1976), orginally published as the first section of his Latin work, *De deo trino*.

Broadly speaking, Dunn follows the theories of Walter Bauer and Ernst Käsemann, both of whom hold that primitive Christianity was a charismatic movement which only gradually hardened into the confessionalism which we call orthodoxy, or early Catholicism. This view has had a number of distinguished advocates, among whom Dunn must be regarded as something of a populariser, but the assumptions on which it rests are far too slender a foundation to bear the weight of the theoretical construction built upon them. Dunn, for example, freely admits the presence of a catholicising tendency within the early Church, but has great difficulty in deciding when and to what extent it separated out from the mass of early christian belief, to make what one might crudely term, a take-over bid. Dunn strengthens his case by relegating the Pastoral Epistles, the Johannine corpus, and Luke-Acts to the last twenty years of the first century, which is very late, to say the least, and by driving as many wedges as possible between these books and the rest of the New Testament. As an example of where this method can lead, we quote from p. 29:

Evidently the author (of 1 John) assumed that he who loves is he who makes a right confession. It is not at all evident what the author would make of the man who displays a Christ-like love and who yet refuses to believe in

44

Christ. The sharp Johannine antithesis provides no answer to the (Christian) 'problem' of the good pagan, the loving atheist. Paul, on the other hand, with his recognition of the divided state of each man and his yearning over unbelieving Israel would at least understand the problem and be able to volunteer some answer. Whereas 1 John has nothing to say.

Gratuitous assumptions of this kind are matched only by Dunn's failure to come to terms with Luke-Acts, which he regards as a paradoxical combination of charisma and confession. How this paradox occurred in a Church which was supposedly being torn into opposing camps along these lines, Dunn is unable to explain. The obvious answer is that such a division is unworkable; charisma and confession belong together at the heart of the Church's faith, and have developed together from the very beginning.

It is true, of course, that we must be exceedingly cautious about making any claims for the various confessional statements found in the New Testament, and we may readily agree with those who argue that dogmatic formulae are not to be found in its pages. This is true, but it does not invalidate the claim that the use of dogmata is consistent with a faith rooted in Scripture. For the difference between Scripture and dogma is to be sought at the level of genre, or form, not at the level of principle. The biblical writers were not trying to be systematic theologians, although they were clearly happy to make propositional statements about God and his activity in Jesus Christ. There is a coherent picture underlying their writings, and by careful piecing together of the evidence we can reconstruct it. It must be remembered, however, that *all* the evidence must be taken into account; it is a fatal mistake to take isolated texts as self-contained and self-explanatory in a way which ignores the witness of other parts, or of the

45

whole. This was the exegetical error of Arius, which is repeated today by those who take the Pauline greetings, for example, as evidence that the early Church was largely binitarian in its theology.

For a more positive evaluation of the relationship between Scripture and dogma we may turn to the Jesuit philosopher and theologian, Bernard Lonergan.[1] Lonergan states clearly that the credal dogmata do not contain anything foreign to Scripture, and explains the difference between them as one of mode. Superficially it might appear that this is the same as our own word genre, and indeed Lonergan does use this term, but the context of his philosophy makes it clear that this is not the case. Lonergan unfortunately ties the development of dogma to his own theories of human consciousness, so that while Scripture supposedly appeals to the 'whole man' and represents a state of undifferentiated consciousness, dogma makes its appeal primarily to the intellect and corresponds to a state of differentiated consciousness. Lonergan therefore represents the passage from *sola Scriptura* to *Scriptura* plus dogma as part of a necessary evolution of religion in the light of the unfolding differentiation of the human mind. It is of course obvious that this evolution has been posited by Lonergan on anthropological, rather than theological grounds, and that it is open to serious criticism from either standpoint. More specifically, there are two points which Lonergan makes which seem to us to be false, or at least highly misleading.

The first is the assumption that Scripture, and especially the Gospels, appeals to the 'whole man' while dogma does not. As he says:

The gospels, and the apostolic writings generally are not just a collection of true propositions, addressed only to the mind of the reader; they teach the truth, but in such a way that they penetrate the sensibility, fire the imagination, engage the affections, touch the heart, open the eyes, attract and impel the will of the reader. Conciliar decrees are totally different: so clearly and so accurately do they declare what is true that they seem to bypass the senses, the feelings and the will, to appeal only to the mind.[2]

It is true that Lonergan later modifies this opposition somewhat, but the fundamental antithesis remains. Lonergan does not seem to have realised, that although Scripture certainly appeals to more than a man's rational faculty, it is nevertheless addressed in the first instance to the mind. Moreover, the strange notion that dogma enlightens man's intellect without penetrating his emotions is refuted, by what we know of early Church history, when according to our sources, the crowds of Alexandria and Constantinople could be whipped into a frenzy over such 'obscurities' as the *homoousion*. Nor does such a distinction correspond with the testimony of later ages. It was John Henry Newman, no less, who confessed to the deeply moving power of the Athanasian Creed, that great hymn to the Holy Trinity, and his witness has been echoed by countless thousands of others through the ages. As with other forms of art and literature, the appreciation of dogma must be learned by patient study and application – but so it is of course with Scripture as well. Lonergan has rooted his distinction in a false premiss, and it must be recast on a different foundation.

The second objection we have to his analysis is his extraordinary statement that the patristic writers, when they stumbled on the notion of dogma, had no idea of the development they were encouraging, and would have been strenuously opposed to it if they had understood its implications. Again, Lonergan has either not realised, or not given sufficient attention to, the fact that dogma, as a form of logical discourse, was already well established in the ancient world before Christianity appeared on the scene. It is true that christian intellectuals were by no means happy with their pagan cultural inheritance, and often sought to avoid it as much as possible, but it cannot be said that they were unaware of it, or insensitive to the charge that the use of philosophical techniques was somehow a corruption of Christianity.

All the evidence indicates that the patristic writers were very sensitive indeed to the issues involved, and that they bent over backwards to maintain not only the teaching of Scripture, but even its vocabulary, as a bulwark against the infiltration of pagan rationalism. But amidst all the heresies and dissensions which rent the early Church there was no one, or at least no one of importance known to us, who disputed the appropriateness of a systematic theology bringing together the logical propositions of the biblical revelation. Even the most radical dissenters, the Marcionites and the Valentinians for example, agreed on this, and sought to produce systems of their own. To point to the Montanists, as some do, as an instance of an anti-dogmatic, charismatic protest movement is ingenuous rather than accurate, as ought to be clear from a work like Tertullian's *Adversus Praxean*. It is not too much to say in fact that the Holy Spirit cult of Montanus was but the logical extension, at a popular level, of the economic trinitarianism then in vogue in the most intellectual circles.

From what has been said so far, it will be clear that modern attempts to divide charisma from confession in the life of the early Church will not work. What is perhaps less clear is the extent to which our own view differs from both Dunn and Lonergan, who in our opinion are fundamentally alike in their understanding of primitive Christianity. Both men regard dogmatic development as a progression from the whole to a part, from an all-embracing faith to a set of intellectual convictions. Admittedly Dunn sees this in negative terms, and Lonergan in positive ones, but the fundamental approach is much the same.

Our own position by contrast, though superficially it may appear similar to Lonergan's, is quite different, in that it rejects the evolutionary theory which underlies his analysis. The emergence of dogmatism as the vehicle of christian theological thought was not a progression in that sense, but an adaptation of the faith to a particular form of expression which proved, and we would wish to argue, still proves, most suitable to it. We would not wish to insist that dogmatism is itself a part of the revelation, still less that a man must fully understand all the nuances of the Athanasian Creed before having any hope of salvation. Dogma is not the gateway to the kingdom of heaven, but rather the blueprint which describes in a concise and systematic fashion what it looks like and where to find the key.

II. ADAPTATION OR EVOLUTION

Bearing this fundamental principle in mind, we turn to consider the development of the dogma of the Trinity. The history of classical trinitarianism is of course well known, and does not need to be retold here in any detail.[3] What we are interested in, is whether the trinitarian formulations of the fourth and fifth centuries conform to the picture of adaptation which we have posited as the chief characteristic of Christian dogmatism, or whether there was some more fundamental evolution which, rightly or wrongly, led the Church away from the orbit of purely biblical thought.

The latter thesis has been most forcefully maintained by Maurice Wiles, who has suggested that classical trinitarianism developed in two distinct historical stages, the second of which used Scripture in a way which contradicted the way it had been interpreted in the first stage, when, says Wiles, 'the primary emphasis of the theologians ... was the demonstration of the distinct existence of the three persons of the godhead. The chief enemy was the popular Monarchianism of a modalist kind which blurred or denied the reality of those distinctions.'[4] In the second stage, however, the issue at stake had changed, and it became necessary to defend the co-equality of the persons against the subordination of Arius. As a result, arguments used in the first stage had to be dropped, and even tacitly repudiated, in the second.

As an example of this, Wiles selects Tertullian's argument in *Adversus Praxean* 14 that the Son is distinct from the Father because he is visible, while the Father is not. Wiles claims that Tertullian had difficulty in maintaining this distinction, and that he contradicted himself within the space of a single chapter, but argues that he nevertheless clung to an idea which in the fourth century proved to be a great embarrassment to theologians who were trying to establish a co-equality of the persons. This made Tertullian's distinction impossible to maintain, says Wiles, and therefore it was repudiated *in toto*.

To begin at the beginning, it must be urged that Wiles is mistaken in his belief that 'the primary emphasis of the theologians of the second and third centuries was the demonstration of the distinct existence of the three persons of the godhead'. On the contrary, it is not difficult to show that the first and fundamental concern of all the patristic writers was to preserve a pure monotheism. In the second century in particular, this was closely linked to the idea that God was the creator of the universe and Father of all mankind. During this period, the fatherhood of God was generally understood in a more or less Judaic way, which also happened to be congenial to certain elements in Greek philosophy, especially

in Stoicism. When we read therefore that God was spoken of
as Father in the writings of the apologists, we must bear in
mind that the term refers to the relationship of God to the
world, and is not being used in a strictly trinitarian sense.

No one will deny that the apologists' conception of God
came from their reading of the Bible, and its validity has
hardly been questioned, but it must be remembered that
they were unable to rest content with a theology which
scarcely distinguished Christianity from Judaism. As
Christians, it was an essential tenet of their belief that God
had somehow become man in Jesus Christ. To explain this,
without compromising their fundamental monotheism, the
apologists appealed to the prologue to John's Gospel, whence
they said that the Logos, which had been latent in the Father
from all eternity, had been generated in the world of time and
space in the person of Jesus Christ. Similarly, though they
did not develop this point, the Holy Spirit had also been in
the Father from all eternity, and had proceeded from him on
the Day of Pentecost.

It will be seen immediately that the theology of the
apologists can only be understood to the extent that we
appreciate their conception of the relationship between
finitude and infinity. For them, the entry of the transcendent
God into the realm of the contingent was somehow produc-
tive of a distinction within the Godhead which had not been
previously manifest. How and why this happened, forms the
basis of their trinitarianism, which is why it is usually called
economic, or dispensational.

It is when we have grasped this point that we may appreciate how significant was the apologists' rejection of modalism.
This heresy, which held that the Son and the Spirit were
merely different names for the Father in the various stages of
his redemptive activity, held a natural appeal for anyone who
thought of God in dispensational terms. Yet, of course, it

would never do. Quite apart from the fact that it would involve the divine becoming not merely involved in, but subject to, the world of contingency, there was the obvious fact that in the Gospels the Son spoke to his Father as to another person, and that he expressly stated that the Holy Spirit would come as *another* comforter, not as the same one with a different name.

Some kind of distinction could therefore be detected between the persons of the Godhead, which went beyond the bounds of the finite, though the precise nature of these distinctions lay beyond the scope of revelation. The apologists were content to affirm the pre-existence of the Logos and of the Spirit in the Father, and did not enquire further into the mystery. We are therefore forced to conclude that what Wiles sees as their primary emphasis was in fact the point at which the theology of the apologists was at its least satisfactory. Their conception of divine fatherhood, and their concentration on the economy of the divine action in the world produced an essentially apophatic response to questions involving the internal relations of the Godhead, even though they understood that some such distinctions must exist.

The inadequacy of the apologists' economic trinitarianism became apparent in the third century when it was challenged, probably unconsciously at first, by both Tertullian and Origen. Wiles makes much of Tertullian as a representative of the first stage of theological enquiry, but caution is required here. Whatever his long-term influence on trinitarian dogmatic formulae may have been, in the short-term it was not as great as Wiles implies. Especially in the East, where Latin theology was generally unknown, it is less than helpful to picture him as a predecessor of Athanasius and the Cappadocians. By the same token, he was not just a Latin apologist, and to treat him as representative of economic trinitarianism in its full flowering is both anachronistic, and somewhat misleading.

Bearing these qualifications in mind, we may look briefly at what Tertullian says about the relationship between the Father and the Son to see whether Wiles is right in his criticisms. Wiles says:

> If the distinction between the Father and the Son lies in the fact that the one is invisible and the other visible, they can hardly be co-equal persons in the one godhead. (Even Tertullian has been conscious of a weakness in his own argument at this point, and having once made it contradicts himself in the same chapter of the *Adversus Praxean* by asserting that the Son, as Spirit and Word of God, is invisible and that the Old Testament records of man who saw God ought to be understood to refer to dreams and visions.) Moreover, the same Johannine texts about the sending and authorizing of the Son by the Father which Tertullian had used to indicate his distinctiveness from the Father were used by the Arians as evidence of his inferiority. Later writers therefore found themselves forced to deny the applicability of such texts to the relation of the Father and the Son altogether . . . Ignoring the fact, therefore, that such an interpretation of those texts was a part of the ground upon which they themselves were standing, they insisted that they did not refer to the relation of the first two persons of the Trinity at all but to the relation of the Father and the incarnate Christ (*op. cit.* pp. 126–7).

If we may take the matter of the texts first, it is not altogether clear exactly which texts Wiles has in mind, but it is surely obvious that with his background of essentially economic trinitarianism, Tertullian saw no incongruity in using texts which referred to the incarnate Christ as evidence to indicate his distinctiveness from the Father. When later writers denied that these texts could be applied to the relation between the Father and the Son, they were not contradicting what Tertullian had said – and let us remind ourselves again that most of these men were almost completely ignorant of Tertullian's thought – but talking about something else, of which Tertullian was only imperfectly aware, viz. the eternal relations within the Godhead.

On this question, it may be tantalising to speculate whether Tertullian believed in the eternal generation of the Son as this was subsequently understood, but it must be remembered that the difficulties raised by sheer anachronism are too great even to allow such a question to be asked. For Tertullian, as for his predecessors, the concept of generation belonged irretrievably to the world of the contingent and therefore could not be applied to an eternal reality within God. But while the generation of the Son within the Godhead could not be called eternal, neither could it be contained within the temporal, since it was a divine reality, and the divine was not bound by time. This solution, which to later minds appears like the most subtle kind of fence-sitting, shows just how intolerable a strain was being put on the economic trinitarian model.

A similar strain may be observed in the matter of the Son's visibility. It is noteworthy that Tertullian never links this to the Incarnation, but discusses the question solely in the light of the divine epiphanies recorded in the Old Testament. He accepts that no man can see the Father, but only the Son who makes himself visible to men. From this he deduces that the Old Testament epiphanies were appearances of the Son, which indicates that he existed as a distinct person before the Incarnation. But the Son, being God, was also by nature invisible, which meant that all talk of seeing him must be understood in an analogical sense. This does not mean, as

Wiles seems to imply, that the visions were a kind of halluci-
nation, but rather that there was a spiritual sight which
enabled specially-gifted men to behold the invisible.
Tertullian does not expressly say so, but it is obvious that
even in the Gospels the knowledge that the incarnate Christ
was the Son of God had been given to Peter by spiritual, not
physical means (Matt. 16.17).

It is surprising that Wiles, in his sketch of trinitarian
development, gives such a prominent place to Tertullian,
whose entry into the mainstream of discussion was tardy and
indirect, but it is even more surprising that he almost
completely overlooks Origen,[5] who by any standard was *the*
central figure in the third century debates, and whose
theological constructions were still immensely influential
long after Nicaea. Origen understood quite clearly that the
central issue for trinitarianism was the question of the
internal relations of the persons of the Godhead, which by
the very nature of God, must be eternal. The Incarnation
could only be the enactment in time of a generation which lay
beyond the temporal – ergo, the Son, had been generated in
and from eternity. But the use of the temporal manifestations
of God as models from which to draw analogies of the eternal
nature of the trinitarian relationships, while it doubtless was
a move in the right direction, had serious drawbacks of its
own which Origen did not fully appreciate. In his earthly life
and work, the Son had obviously been in submission to the
Father. It followed, therefore, that submission was a basic
ingredient of his divine personhood – hence the Son was
eternally subordinate to the Father.

At the deepest level, what Origen did was to bring into the
open the question of how the person and the work of the
members of the Godhead were connected. Was it the need for
their redemptive function which caused the generation of the
Son and the procession of the Spirit, or was it as a result of

this pre-existing fact that they were able to perform the redemptive tasks allotted to them? This question had of course been equally fundamental to the theology of the apologists, but their inability to divorce the concept of generation from the realm of contingency prevented them from analysing the problem on the level of pure being. Origen's progression from an economic trinitarianism whose bias was basically functional to a more ontological conception will be seen by many as a change of direction, but in fact it was a breakthrough to a level of discourse which had been implicit all along.

The lesson of the second century was that any doctrine of the Trinity which rested on the temporal manifestations of the Godhead would sooner or later be shaped into modalism or adoptionism, neither of which did justice to the New Testament conception of the relationship between Father and Son. To account for this adequately it was necessary to probe beyond what Jesus did and examine who he was, not merely in himself, since his divinity was seldom questioned, but also in relation to the Father. Origen believed, and subsequent writers set out to prove, that an ontological christology was not only required by the facts of trinitarian logic but also that it was profoundly embedded in the teaching of the New Testament. In modern times of course this view has been seriously challenged, even by some who would wish to uphold the trinitarianism of the creeds. A subject of such magnitude clearly cannot be dealt with here in any detail, but it is safe to say that a middle position like the one just outlined will not be tenable for long, and the more radical theologians who have rejected it are perfectly logical in their analysis. Unless one believes that the christology of the New Testament is fundamentally ontological, then it seems most unlikely that classical trinitarianism will ever make much sense. The options now, as in Origen's time, are a form of modalism or of adoptionism, and the recent work of the more radical scholars would seem to indicate that it is the latter which is proving the greater attraction at the present time.

To return to Origen, however, his work made it impossible for subsequent writers to ignore the question of divine being, and discussion inevitably gravitated in that direction. The intersection of the finite with the infinite was certainly not lost sight of, but it was put in context as theologians realised more clearly that it was the inner nature of the latter which would determine its operations on and within the former. In this respect, Origen's work was fundamental for all subsequent debate.

The immediate difficulty with his thought, however, was that his appreciation of the significance of the divine being was combined with a particular doctrine of hierarchy within the Godhead. He apparently never realised that if the eternal generation of the Son were acknowledged, then it would be impossible to maintain that he was in any way inferior to the Father in deity. It may seem daring to suggest that Arianism was doomed to failure from the start, but so it almost certainly was. No heresy before or since has ever received such powerful external support, but nothing could salvage it from its basic theological dilemma. If the Son was not eternally generate, then there must have been a time when he was not, but since he was born within the Godhead, his birth was not subject to time. It was therefore nonsense, as the orthodox pointed out, to claim that there had been a time when the Son had not existed. But if the Son was eternally generate, then he was equal to the Father, since his generation had no bearing on the nature of his being.

Arianism certainly led to a renewed outburst of theological activity, but this fact should not mislead us. Its long-term effect was to confirm the inescapable, rather than to initiate any new advance in christian doctrine. The work of the Cappadocians in particular, was a detailed elaboration of issues whose main lines had been settled long before, and it is doubtful whether their achievement would have been possible otherwise. As they explained it, the persons of the Godhead were distinct but inseparable, and the same was true of their work. Thus while the sacrifice of the cross was the work of the Son offered to the Father, to the world it was the work of the triune God, since in Christ the fullness of the Godhead dwelt bodily. The Cappadocians could therefore claim that *opera trinitatis ad extra sunt indivisa*, not, as Wiles seems to imagine, as a hidden concession to modalism, but as the mature reflection of true biblical teaching about three persons in one God. To them it was clear that the work of each person was the common work of all three, without however, detracting from the specific aspects attributed to each one. Thus it was the Son, not the Father nor the Spirit, who suffered in a human body on the cross to accomplish the reconciliation between God and man; and the Spirit, not the Father nor the Son, who descended on the apostles at Pentecost. Yet the Son did not act independently of the Father and the Spirit, nor did the Spirit come down apart from the Father and the Son. The fullness of God was present and active in both great, typical works in a way which the human mind can perceive yet never fully understand.

Thus far we have said very little about the Holy Spirit, who is in many ways the most problematic member of the Trinity. Our silence reflects the course of trinitarian theology in the ante-Nicene period, for although his presence was always keenly felt, his person and work were seldom discussed in any detail. The main reason for this is probably that for a long time trinitarian theology was little more than a by-product of christology, which claimed by far the larger share of attention. When, however, the person and work of the Son were

firmly anchored in the context of his eternal relation to the
Father, the way was opened up to a fuller appreciation of the
Holy Spirit. His work as the witness to Christ and the sancti-
fier of the people of God had always been recognised in the
Church, though never developed in its trinitarian context.
Even Tertullian, who showed as great an awareness of the
Spirit's work as anyone in the early Church, had little to say
on this point.[6]

The full development of a doctrine of the Spirit was left to
the Cappadocians and later, Augustine, who discarded the
last vestiges of economic trinitarianism and stressed the full,
eternal co-equality of the persons. Unfortunately, his work
never circulated in the East, and this was to prove fateful in
the long struggles over the double procession of the Spirit,
ironically the most enduring and the most bitter of all the
trinitarian debates. We have not the space here to elaborate a
defence of the *filioque,* though we have no doubt that it must
be defended, but would only point out that much of the
debate hinges on the doctrine of the Father, an aspect of
trinitarianism which to this day remains remarkably unexplored.[7] In particular, does his rôle as the Fountainhead of
Deity exclude the possibility of the Spirit's procession from
the Son?

Our study began with the nature of dogma, and from there
moved on to consider the development of classical trinitarianism. It remains now to reflect briefly on the continuing
validity of all this in the light of our present circumstances.
Here it will be instructive to quote yet again from Maurice
Wiles, who after ranging through the weaknesses (as he sees
them) of the doctrine, delivers what he supposes will be the
coup de grâce: 'Patristic reasoning about the Trinity', he says,
'can only be saved from the charge of inconsistency by allow-
ing that it is grounded on an appeal to Scripture of a kind

which is totally at variance with one that would find general acceptance in the modern world'.[8]

Here as elsewhere, Wiles does not bother to be precise as to what he means by an appeal to Scripture which is no longer acceptable, and this inevitably makes it difficult to answer his charge. At one level, we may agree that the Fathers of the Church had an amusing, if at times irritating, propensity for finding doctrines where they ought not, and the notorious Proverbs 8.22 springs immediately to mind. Of course, it must be remembered that this verse was not used to support orthodox claims; on the contrary, it was a major weapon in the hands of the Arians. Modern critics may deplore the inability of Athanasius to appreciate just how irrelevant a text it was, but no one can accuse him, or anyone else for that matter, of building a doctrine of the Trinity on it, or on passages like it.

More to the point are the passages from John's Gospel which, on the surface at least, plainly support the classical position. Wiles rejects them, apparently on the ground that they are unhistorical. This, of course, is a matter of opinion, but we should not be too dismayed by charges of this kind. For one thing, historicity in the strict sense is a matter of secondary importance, since the statements involved are not themselves historical. In discussing a statement like 'I and the Father are one' it is of only marginal interest to discover when, where and even why Jesus said, or was supposed to have said it. Much more important is the degree of truth it contains; and this is a rather different question.

It may be that the analogical interpretation of such texts needs to be reworked or abandoned, but if so, the case has yet to be made. The contemporary validity of patristic trinitarianism is bound up with our whole understanding of the nature of truth, and the accuracy with which Holy Scripture can and does convey the truth in the language of men. If by an unacceptable view of the Bible, Wiles means primarily the doctrine of its divine character as revelation of God, then we may readily agree that he has put his finger on the heart of the problem. For in the final analysis it is the validity of our epistemology, which is summed up in the doctrine of Scripture, which will determine the validity of the rest.

Diocese of Chelmsford   GERALD LEWIS BRAY

NOTES

1. *Editorial note:* The reader will find that Hugo Meynell takes a different attitude to Lonergan's views. See further Peter Toon, *The Development Doctrine in the Church* (Grand Rapids, 1979), ch. 7.
2. B. Lonergan, *The Way to Nicea* (London, 1976), p. 1.
3. See e.g. J. N. D. Kelly, *Early Christian Doctrine* (London, 4th edn., 1977).
4. Maurice Wiles, *The Making of Christian Doctrine* (Cambridge, 1967), p. 124.
5. Origen is not mentioned at all in the passage we are at present discussing, and figures only marginally in his older, but fuller treatment, 'Some Reflections on the Origins of the Doctrine of the Trinity', *J.T.S.* n.s. 8, 1957, pp. 92–106.
6. Cf. esp. *Adversus Praxean*, which despite its professed aim to vindicate the Paraclete as well as combat patripassianism, does the latter far more thoroughly than the former.
7. *Editorial note:* See further chapter five.
8. M. Wiles, op. cit., p. 129.

CHAPTER FIVE

The *Filioque* Clause[1]

The '*filioque* clause' is to be found in the version of the Nicene
Creed which is generally used in the Roman Catholic and
other Western Churches. '*Filioque*' is the Latin for 'and from
the Son', and the clause comes in the section of the Creed
which deals with the 'procession', or 'coming forth' of the
Holy Spirit:

> And I believe in the Holy Ghost, the Lord, and Giver of
> Life, who proceeds from the Father AND THE SON, who
> with the Father and the Son together is worshipped and
> glorified, who spoke by the prophets.

This clause was not part of the original wording of the Creed,
which dates from the fourth century. Nor was it presented or
approved at the ancient Ecumenical Councils which established the Nicene Creed as the standard of orthodox christian
faith. It was only later, and only in the Western Church, that
it came to be accepted. To this day, the Eastern Orthodox
Churches preserve the original wording, 'who proceeds from
the Father, who with the Father and the Son together is
worshipped and glorified . . .' The difference may appear a
very minor one but it led to much conflict between East and
West and was one significant cause of the estrangement
between them which produced in the eleventh century the
separation that still continues today. In recent ecumenical

62

dialogue it has come again to the fore as a topic demanding
attention.

I. THE INCLUSION OF THE CLAUSE IN THE NICENE CREED

The Nicene Creed holds a unique place among all the creeds
and confessions formulated through the centuries. It includes, in modified form, the main elements of the creed
framed by the Council of Nicaea – the first Ecumenical
Council – in AD 325. As a whole, however, it dates from the
Second Council, held at Constantinople in 381. The name
'Nicene Creed' is thus not strictly accurate, but is more or
less universally used. The Creed's authority as the classic
statement of orthodox christian belief was affirmed by the
Fourth Council at Chalcedon in 451, and accepted by the
Church in both East and West. While there were many other
creeds in the ancient Church, none of them, apart from the
original creed of Nicea itself, was given this measure of
conciliar approval or so universally received. Even the so-
called Apostles' Creed in its present form is a much later
formulation, dating from about the eighth century; and it is
in fact a Western creed which was never formally accepted
by the Eastern Church.[2]

In affirming that the Holy Spirit 'proceeds from the
Father', the framers of the Nicene Creed at Constantinople
were emphasising that the Spirit is nothing less than God. As
the Son is 'begotten' from the Father, and therefore 'God
from God', so the Spirit 'proceeds' from the Father. This,
however, leaves room for a further question: is there also a
connexion between the Son and the Spirit? Some of the Greek
Fathers could say that the Spirit proceeds 'from the Father
through the Son', and this way of putting'the matter has
traditionally been preferred by the Eastern Church. It has
not, however, led to the addition of 'through the Son' in the

Nicene Creed in the East. Some of the Latin Fathers on the other hand went further and said that the Spirit proceeds 'from the Father and the Son'. This understanding was developed in detail by St Augustine in the early fifth century – e.g. in his *De Trinitate* xv.xvii.29. He described the Holy Spirit as the 'bond of love' (*vinculum caritatis*) between the Father and the Son, and so as 'proceeding' from both. At the same time, Augustine was careful to point out that he proceeds *principally* from the Father: the Father is the source and origin of the Son and of the Spirit, and therefore also of the Spirit's procession from the Son. The Spirit proceeds directly from the Father, and also indirectly from the Father in proceeding from the Son. Augustine's thought was little known or appreciated in the Greek East, but had an enormous influence in the West. His conception of the 'double procession of the Spirit', as it may be called, came to be more or less universally accepted in the Western Church; it was re-expressed in the misnamed 'Athanasian Creed', which came into wide circulation in the West in the sixth century; and it eventually led to the insertion of the *filioque* clause in the Nicene Creed itself, though this only came about by easy stages through long centuries.[3]

In 589, on the conversion of King Reccared from Arianism, the Council of Toledo (which was a local, not an ecumenical council) stated that 'the Holy Spirit is to be confessed by us and preached as proceeding from the Father and the Son (*et a filio*)'.[4] It is possible that the prime motive of this statement was to emphasise the full divinity of the Son – which Arianism denied – but it may equally be that those present at the council simply took it for granted that the Spirit proceeds from the Son as well as from the Father. It is unlikely that this council actually altered the wording of the Nicene Creed itself; but in the following centuries, versions of the Creed including the *filioque* clause came to be used quite widely in the West, especially in Spain and France. During the reign of Pope Leo III (795–816) the Emperor Charlemagne attempted to impose the addition throughout the Church; but Leo, while agreeing with the theology of the *filioque*, refused to sanction any interference with the wording of the Creed. This did not, however, put an end to the debate, or to the pressure in favour of the change; and two centuries later, probably in 1014, Pope Benedict VIII finally approved the expansion of the Creed at the same time as the singing of the Creed was incorporated in the liturgy of the Mass in Rome. This helped to pave the way for the rupture between the Eastern and Western Church which followed forty years later, in 1054. There had been debate and controversy between East and West on the point in the preceding centuries – notably when Photius was Patriarch of Constantinople in 858–867 and 878–886 – but at that stage the Roman Popes still held to Leo's position and maintained the Creed unaltered. Benedict's action, in the eyes of the East, brought matters to a more serious, even disastrous head. In the West, on the other hand, some of the very ablest theologians set out to defend and justify both the theology of the *filioque* and its insertion into the Creed. The main contributions were those of St Anselm in his *De Processione Spiritus Sancti* and St Thomas Aquinas in his *Summa Theologiae* I, *quaestio* 36. The core of their argument (though it was worked out in a variety of complex ways) was that if the Trinity were not to dissolve into an undifferentiated unity, nor fragment into unrelated parts, there must be a fundamental relationship between the Son and the Spirit which would both link them and distinguish them from each other. This relationship was what the *filioque* described.

Attempts were made to reconcile East and West at the Councils of Lyons (1274) and Florence (1439). At Lyons it was explained that the *filioque* did not mean that the Spirit had two separate and distinct sources in the Father and the Son. Rather, 'he proceeds eternally from the Father and the Son, not as if from two sources, but as from a single source, not by two breathings, but by a single breathing' (DS §850). At Florence, this clarification was repeated; and it was further added that the formula 'through the Son' familiar to the Greeks tended towards the same meaning as the *filioque* itself (DS §1301). These explanations did not in the end satisfy the Eastern Church, and the 'agreement' reached at these Councils proved short-lived.

Although the Reformation brought some exploratory contacts between some of the Reformers and the Eastern Orthodox, the Churches of the Reformation generally held to the Western understanding expressed in the *filioque*. Here, as in so many other areas, the heritage of earlier Western theology was preserved without serious question, and the Creed, where it continued to be used, still included the *filioque* clause.

II. THREE CENTRAL ISSUES

In the debate about the *filioque* three chief questions have arisen. First of all, can it be justified by the teaching of the Bible, and particularly of the New Testament? That the Holy Spirit 'proceeds from the Father' is directly stated in John 15.26, the text which is echoed in the original wording of the Creed. But there is no equally simple and clear scriptural statement that he also proceeds 'from the Son'. Second, did the Western Church in the person of Benedict VIII have the authority to expand the Creed whose terms had been decided by an Ecumenical Council? The Eastern Orthodox view is that it did not, and the unilateral alteration of the Creed by the West has itself been strongly criticised by the East. Third, does the theology of the *filioque* express a proper understanding of the Trinity? Here again, East and West have been deeply divided.

1. The Filioque and Scripture

Before asking whether the *filioque* is supported by the witness of Scripture, it is as well first to consider what kind of exegetical basis for a theological formulation of this sort can properly be looked for. It cannot simply be a matter of searching to see whether the Spirit is anywhere said to 'proceed from the Son' as well as 'from the Father'. Calvin's remarks on the term 'person' apply equally to the *filioque*:

> If they call it a foreign term because it cannot be pointed out in Scripture in so many syllables, they certainly impose an unjust law – a law which would condemn every interpretation of Scripture that is not composed of other words of Scripture.[5]

The question must rather be whether the over-all shape and force of what the Bible has to say about the relation between Christ and the Spirit affords support for what the *filioque* affirms; and conversely, whether the *filioque* opens up and strengthens a dogmatic theology of the Trinity which functions as dogmatic theology ought – namely to deepen our grasp of that of which the Bible speaks. These are issues in the field of dogmatics rather than of biblical criticism. The *filioque* cannot be simply lifted out of its context in the doctrine of the Trinity and carried off on its own to be measured against the Bible. It is possible, however, to note points in Scripture which are especially relevant for the dogmatic evaluation of the *filioque*.

The most significant of these points is the connexion between Jesus and the Spirit, both during his earthly life and after his resurrection. It must be admitted that just as there are diverse christologies in the New Testament, so too there are diverse theologies of the Spirit which ought not to be run together in an artificial synthesis. They can, however, be held together in a broad over-all pattern which appears in part in various places in the New Testament, and is most coherently articulated in the Gospel of John. The Spirit is the power of the divine life which was present and at work in Jesus himself, and through his life, death and resurrection is given by him to his disciples. The respective emphases of the Synoptic Gospels upon the role of the Spirit in Jesus' life and ministry and of Paul and Acts on his activity in the early Church, while they have their own distinctive tone and colouring, fit into this broad scheme. Jesus is the one on whom the Spirit rests; he is the one who gives the Spirit; the Spirit is the Spirit of Christ; and in the Spirit Christ himself is present among his people.

This connexion between Jesus and the Spirit is so fundamental to the New Testament teaching that the dogmatic understanding of the Trinity must take account of it. A doctrine of the Trinity which sees no intrinsic connexion between the person of the Son and that of the Spirit lays itself open to the charge of having cut loose from its moorings. The understanding expressed in the *filioque* is not open to that charge. Equally, however, the connexion could be expressed in other ways, for example, by 'from the Father through the Son'. Other than exegetical considerations must be drawn in if we are to travel further into the question: we shall return to it below.

2. The Expansion of the Creed
Behind the Eastern appeal to the original wording of the Nicene Creed lies the immense veneration with which the Eastern Orthodox Churches regard the ancient Ecumenical Councils. These are seen as having been inspired by the Holy

Spirit to guide and express the mind of the universal Church. Consequently, only another Council with the same standing and authority could modify or add to what they had defined.

This attitude to the Councils is rather different from those of the Roman Catholic Church on the one hand and the various Churches of the Reformation on the other. The Roman Catholic Church looks on the early Councils in much the same light as does the East; but it also holds that the same authority which they exercised is preserved in its continuing *magisterium*, in the doctrinal tradition laid down in subsequent Western councils, and supremely in the person of the Pope himself.[6] It cannot therefore accept that Benedict VIII was exceeding his authority when he sanctioned the addition of the *filioque* to the Creed. (By the same token, however, it would presumably be possible for a future Pope or Council to exercise the same authority and restore the original wording.) The Churches of the Reformation, whether Lutheran, Reformed, Anglican or other, generally have yet a different view. While the Reformers did commonly appeal to the early Church against later developments, and to this extent might appear to sympathise with the Eastern rather than the Roman Catholic approach, they were very far from ascribing to the Ecumenical Councils the status which they possess in Eastern Orthodox theology. They insisted rather on the primacy and authority of Scripture and subordinated subsequent tradition and doctrinal development to it. In this horizon, the authority of the ancient Councils was relative rather than absolute. Certainly, there is a wide spectrum of attitudes to the early Church and its Councils in the Churches of the Reformation today. At one end of the scale is a very 'high' view of the authority of antiquity, a view particularly prominent in some strands of the Anglican communion (though not only there). In its most intense form, this becomes practically indistinguishable from the

Eastern Orthodox or Roman Catholic outlook. At the other end of the scale, the early Church is virtually ignored, and no significant authority at all ascribed to the Ecumenical Councils. If all the Churches of the Reformation are taken together, there is little doubt that the centre of gravity lies towards the 'low' rather than the 'high' end. This makes it difficult for many of the Reformation Churches fully to appreciate or sympathise with the Eastern Orthodox feeling about the addition of the *filioque* to the Creed. The general, though not universal, view would rather be that the alteration of the text approved by an Ecumenical Council is not in itself *necessarily* wrong or unjustifiable. This attitude is if anything reinforced by the fact that in many of these churches today the Nicene Creed itself is only rarely used, if used at all.

There is, however, another side to the matter. To the extent that the Creed is used in the churches of the Reformation, it is seen as a classical expression of the faith of the Church Universal in past and present. It is not the private possession of any one church, but belongs to the Church as a whole. From this standpoint, and especially in the new ecumenical climate of the twentieth century, the insistence of the Western Church on adding to the Creed which it shared with the East, and on doing so in the teeth of the Eastern objections, can quite properly be seen as an offence against charity and unity, regardless of the particular issue of conciliar authority. It is not necessary to accept the Eastern Orthodox evaluation of the ancient Councils in order to admit that the inclusion of the *filioque* clause in the Creed has become an unfortunate and regrettable barrier to ecumenical understanding. Where the force of this argument is felt, the possibility of returning to the original wording of the Creed suggests itself as a step towards a fuller reconciliation between the Eastern and Western traditions. The matter of the wording of the Creed can thus be distinguished, if not wholly separated, from the question of the theology of the *filioque*, to which we now turn.

3. The Filioque and the Doctrine of the Trinity
The controversy over the *filioque* reflects what has been a real difference in approach to the understanding of the Trinity in East and West. There is certainly no disagreement as to the fundamentals of the doctrine. East and West alike recognise that in God there are three 'persons' or 'hypostases' or 'modes of being' but a single 'essence' or 'substance' or 'nature'. They agree in rejecting Tritheism (which would make the Father, Son and Spirit three distinct individual 'gods'), and Sabellianism (which would treat them merely as three interchangeable aspects or facets of a single, essentially undifferentiated divine being). Both hold that God is 'three in one and one in three'.

Traditionally, however, East and West from the early centuries onwards have tended to approach this unity-in-trinity from opposite sides.[7] The East has characteristically emphasised the irreducible distinctiveness of the three persons; the West, the unbreakable oneness of the shared divine nature. This in turn has issued in contrasting conceptions of the key to the unity of God. The East has generally found that key in the fact that the Son and Spirit derive their being from the Father: the Father, as the unique source and origin of both Son and Spirit, is the guarantor of the divine oneness. The West has looked rather to the one divinity shared and expressed alike by Father, Son, and Spirit.

These different approaches emerge in the medieval conflict between the Western affirmation of the *filioque,* and the East's rejection of it. To the West it has seemed that the three persons must have as much as possible in common: therefore the Father and the Son have it in common that the Holy Spirit proceeds from both. Further, because, as it were, of the pressure towards unity of the one divine nature, there must be a relation between the Son and Spirit comparable to that between each of them and the Father: unless the Spirit is 'from the Son', his being and that of the Son may appear to dissolve into each other. Thus, in the line of thought developed by Anselm and Aquinas, the *filioque* operates both to bind and to distinguish the second and third persons of the Trinity. To the East, by contrast, the *filioque* appeared to split up the being of God by setting up two distinct sources of divinity in the Father *and* in the Son. Western denials of this inference – as at the Councils of Lyons and of Florence – were felt by the East to be unconvincing, and also to risk the additional mistake of fusing the Father and the Son together in the 'single breathing' by which they produce the Spirit. Over against the West's holding together of the Father and the Son as the source of the Spirit, the East came to insist that so far as the origin of his being is concerned, the Spirit proceeds from the Father alone. It did not thereby mean that there was no connexion between Son and the Spirit, but it described the connexion in different terms. Relying on the distinction between the divine *essence* and the divine *energies* – a distinction which was finally crystallised in the work of the fourteenth century theologian Gregory Palamas, though it had a long history before then – Eastern theology established the link between the Son and Spirit at the level of the energies: it is in the Son that the Spirit 'shines out' as the brightness of the Uncreated Light. In this way it sought to *co-ordinate* the Spirit with the Son instead of *subordinating* the Spirit to the Son in the fashion which it believed the Western approach implied; and at the same time to preserve the uniqueness of the Father as the sole source of both.

It is with this divergence between the Eastern and Western approaches to the doctrine of the Trinity that the primary theological issues involved in the *filioque* debate arise. These issues are, not surprisingly, exceedingly complex, but some at least of them can be mentioned as arising in the modern discussion.

III. THE MODERN DISCUSSION

In modern times a variety of positions on the *filioque* have been taken up in East and West. Over eighty years ago the Russian Orthodox theologian V. V. Bolotov published a series of theses in which he inclined to the view that the *filioque* could be interpreted in a sense acceptable to the East,[8] as broadly equivalent to 'through the Son'. A much more critical stance was adopted subsequently by Vladimir Lossky, who maintained that the *filioque* as traditionally understood and defended in the West was in effect Sabellian, and moreover, that it was the root cause of a whole catalogue of other Western errors – Christomonism, a legalistic understanding of the Church, the loss of an eschatological perspective among them – which could all in his view be traced back to the subordination of the person and activity of the Spirit to those of the Son.[9] In the West, the *filioque* has had enthusiastic defenders, including not only Roman Catholic theologians but also Karl Barth,[10] and equally enthusiastic critics.[11] In the last few years, however, the centre of attention has tended to shift towards the question whether East and West together could move to a closer understanding. In 1978 the Faith and Order Commission of the World Council of Churches launched an ecumenical theological study of the *filioque* which may possibly issue in a suggestion that member churches should consider removing the *filioque* clause from the Creed. The same suggestion is currently being debated in the Church of England in the wake of *The Moscow Statement* agreed by representatives of the Anglican and Orthodox communions in July/August 1976.[12] As we have seen, the

73

matter of the wording of the Creed can to some extent be detached from that of the *filioque* theology, though in the longer run the theological question will have to be settled as well if there is to be a real and deep agreement between East and West. Among the most important aspects of that question are the following:

i) There does appear to be some basis for the criticism that the *filioque* as understood and defended in medieval theology does not sufficiently differentiate between the Father and the Son. That line of thinking, represented by Anselm and Aquinas, is significantly different from the earlier view of Augustine, who saw the Spirit as proceeding *principally* from the Father. It is also open to serious question: can the Father and the Son together be equated as producing the Spirit by a 'single breathing'? Does the Spirit stand in the same relation to the Son as to the Father? May there not even be ground for some suspicion that the line of argument developed by Anselm was by way of being a rationalisation and justification for what had already been decided by papal authority?

ii) On the other hand, the traditional Eastern distinction between the divine essence and the divine energies, and the linking of the Spirit with the Son at the second of these levels rather than the first, is equally dubious. It paves the way for a distinction between the 'temporal mission' of the Spirit, in which he is the Spirit of Christ, and his eternal being, in which he is the Spirit proceeding solely from the Father. This, however, drives a wedge between God's being as in himself and his being as towards us, between the 'immanent' and 'economic' Trinity. That is the very thing which much recent Western theology has been rightly concerned to avoid doing, and it is doubtful if the essence/energy distinction, in this application, can be made acceptable to it.

iii) One suggestion which is currently being debated in various quarters is that the Spirit should be seen as 'proceeding from the Father' with the rider that the Father, as Father, is *Father of the Son* rather than simply 'the source, principle and cause of divinity' (as the East has tended to describe him). The procession of the Spirit would then be recognised as standing in some connexion with the 'begetting' of the Son by the Father, and so with the relation between the Father and the Son. It still remains to be seen, however, whether this suggestion can be satisfactorily developed. Much may depend on whether it is looked upon merely as a means of patching together the distinctive Eastern and Western emphases – in which case it may not succeed – or found to open up a more adequate common understanding of the triune being of God which leads on beyond the established traditional theologies. In this connexion, another important question is likely to be whether this approach can link up constructively with the renewed concern for pneumatology arising out of the charismatic movements and assist in the search which some in these movements are making for a fuller christological and trinitarian horizon in which to see and share in the life of the Spirit.[13]

New College   ALASDAIR HERON
Edinburgh

NOTES

1. Part of the material in this paper is taken, with some alterations, from a Report of the Church of Scotland Panel on Doctrine to the 1979

General Assembly. Permission to use this material is gratefully acknowledged.

2. On the history of the development of the creeds, see J. N. D. Kelly, *Early Christian Creeds* (London, 3rd edn. 1972).

3. See e.g. Kelly, op. cit.; H. B. Swete, *On the History of the Doctrine of the Procession of the Holy Spirit* (Cambridge, 1876) and *The Holy Spirit in the Ancient Church* (London, 1912); H. W. Jones, *The Holy Spirit in the Medieval Church* (London, 1922); the standard histories of doctrine; and, most recently, R. Haugh, *Photius and the Carolingians, The Trinitarian Controversy* (Nordland Publishing Co., Belmont, Mass., 1975).

4. Denzinger – Schönmetzer, *Enchiridion Symbolorum* . . . 34th edn. 1967, § 470. (Hereafter referred to as DS.)

5. Calvin, *Institute* I.xiii.3.

6. The superiority of the Pope even over councils has been maintained in the Roman Catholic Church since the Decree *Exsecrabilis* of 1460, DS § 1375.

7. For a somewhat fuller discussion of the different Eastern and Western approaches to the Trinity as bearing upon the *filioque*, may I refer to my article, ' "Who proceedeth from the Father and the Son." The Problem of the *Filioque*'. *Scottish Journal of Theology* 24 (1971), pp. 149–66.

8. 'Thesen Ueber das *Filioque* von einem russischen Theologen', *Revue Internationale de Théologie* 6 (1898), pp. 681–712. Bolotov also held that the *filioque* was a *theologoumenon*, that is, a matter of legitimate theological opinion, rather than a point of doctrine on which all must agree. This 'moderate' approach has been followed by some other Orthodox thinkers, and contrasts with the more 'radical' position of Lossky and his followers.

9. V. Lossky, *The Mystical Theology of the Eastern Church* (London, 1957); 'The Procession of the Holy Spirit in Orthodox Triadology', *Eastern Churches Quarterly* 7.2 (1948), pp. 31–53.

10. Barth, *Church Dogmatics* I.1 § 12, 2.3. See also Bernard Leeming, 'Orthodox-Catholic Relations', in E. L. B. Fry and A. H. Armstrong, *Rediscovering Eastern Christianity. Essays in Memory of Dom Bede Winslow* (London, 1963), pp. 15–50.

11. E.g. G. S. Hendry, *The Holy Spirit in Christian Theology* (London, 1965), pp. 45–52, a critique of Barth, which concludes that 'the *filioque* is a false solution to a real problem'.

12. The Report to the Church of Scotland General Assembly from which

this paper is partly drawn suggests that the Church of Scotland should also be prepared to move in this direction, in consultation with other Churches.

13. E.g. T. A. Smail, *Reflected Glory. The Spirit in Christ and Christians* (London, 1975).

CHAPTER SIX

Karl Barth

In their Preface to the retranslation of volume I/1 of Barth's *Church Dogmatics* G. W. Bromiley and T. F. Torrance draw attention to the earlier translator's comment, that this work contains 'undoubtedly the greatest treatise on the Trinity since the Reformation'. Whereas the late Professor G. T. Thomson only referred back to the Reformation, Bromiley and Torrance go further, and make the tentative claim that it is only with Augustine that we meet the equal of Barth. The basis of such a grandiose claim is not merely that of extent or intellectual complexity, but is, according to Barth's commentators, the over-all redirection of theology that his doctrine of the Trinity is said to have achieved. In other words Barth's undoubted redirection of theological interest to the doctrine of the Trinity was, and is, of global theological importance, inasmuch as it presents a challenge to the fundamental and persistent denigration of the Trinity, as a mere problematical implication of biblical evidence. Besides this, Barth sought to reform christian theological endeavour between, and apart from, the Scylla of the anthropological and subjective starting-point of modernistic Protestantism and the Charybdis of Roman Catholic medieval thought, ostensibly with its shared notion of being, participated in by both man and God. In other words the Trinity itself is the authentic power-house of theology from which radiates the true energy of christian revelation. Indeed, in the words of the Preface, 'the doctrine of the Trinity itself belongs to the

very basis of the christian faith and constitutes the fundamental grammar of dogmatic theology'.[1]

It is important to distinguish between what Barth sets out
to achieve, and claims made on behalf of his work by others.
What shall be attempted in this brief study is to show first
how Barth develops his doctrine of the Trinity in volume I/1
of the *Church Dogmatics*, and then, second, how this basis
underlies the vast structure of the whole work. On this basis
it is possible to advance some tentative comments upon the
over-all nature and structure of this presentation of the
doctrine of the Trinity.

I. THE DOCTRINE OF THE TRINITY

At the very outset a basic contrast may be drawn between the
so-called father of modern theology, Friedrich Schleiermacher, who places the doctrine of the Trinity in an
appendix to *The Christian Faith*,[2] and Barth, who begins with
this conception. The difference of placement is no mere
formal characteristic, because for the former the Trinity is an
incidental rationalisation of the christian experience of God,
whereas for the latter the Trinity is utterly fundamental,
indeed the very distinctiveness of Christianity is constituted
by this datum.[3] Barth's arrival at this starting-point was not
sudden or arbitrary, and his development may be studied
elsewhere. In essence, however, he moved from the Protestant Liberalism characteristic of nineteenth century
German thought (epitomised by Adolf von Harnack, Barth's
own teacher in the early years of this century) to the so-called
'dialectical theology' of the second edition of his commentary
upon the Epistle to the Romans.[4] In this latter work Barth
systematically destroyed the theological basis of any easy
accommodation between Christianity and contemporary
culture by the exploitation of a radical disjunction between

the divine and human spheres of being. The 'infinite quali-
tative distinction' between eternity and time, infinite and
finite existence, which Barth borrowed from Kierkegaard,
was interpreted in such a way that crisis and paradox
displaced mediation and synthesis. The divine realm confronted and overwhelmed the human, God's Word came as
the annihilator of any human pretension based upon any
immanent theological point of contact between God and
man. The annihilation was so complete as to threaten the
whole of theology with its own reduction; for the possibility of
positive relation essential to both a stable christology and
doctrine of creation was threatened by the total nature of the
crisis of confrontation. In the period between the second
edition of *Romans* and the first volume of the *Church Dogmatics*
Barth explored the possibility of new theological starting-
points and so the latter in its positive aspects is the culmi-
nation of a dramatic series of developments.[5]

Positively Barth combined his interpretation of Anselm's
theological method in the *Proslogion*, the notion of 'faith
seeking understanding' and the notion that God himself
provides a rational authentication of language about him in
the 'analogy of faith', with the structural method of Protestant scholasticism and its uninhibited exploitation of
systematically related theological *loci* or points of focus.
These two sets of factors allow Barth to extrapolate from
fundamental theological data, upon the assumption that
there is in fact a single truth (albeit multiplex in appearance),
which provides the basis of all such so-called analogical
derivation. In other words there is no speculative exploration
made in the hope of locating and isolating theological truth.
On the contrary God has acted, acts and will continue to act
in Jesus Christ. God's act in Jesus Christ is not therefore a
surmise but is a primal ontological datum apart from which
any talk of Christianity or revelation is at best misleading

and at worst a damnable perversion. God's act in Jesus
Christ is not merely the exclusive source of the knowledge of
God but also supremely inclusive, for in it the Trinity of God
is revealed and along with this the total theological potential
of christian dogma. To be more explicit it may with justice be
said that the act of God in Jesus Christ unites the Godward
and trinitarian dimension of the divine being with the
expression of that being *vis à vis* man and history in the
doctrines of creation and reconciliation. The doctrine of the
Trinity is, in Barth's theology, the divine being in revealing
action: God is in Trinity insofar as he is in Jesus Christ.

How then does Barth understand and explicate the
Trinity as the 'immediate implicate of revelation'? The
initial presupposition is that the 'proper content of christian
language about God' is ascertainable by man and that, in
consequence 'language about God has the proper content,
when it conforms to the essence of the Church, i.e. to Jesus
Christ' according to what Barth terms the 'analogy of faith'.[6]
Jesus Christ, the 'proper content' of christian language about
God and thus christian theology, is not to be developed by
the extrapolation of the propositions contained either in Holy
Scripture (as in a Protestant biblicism) or in a 'deposit of
faith' (the truths ostensibly consigned to the Catholic
Church by the Apostles) but by an explication of the actual
contemporaneity of God in Christ now. The Trinity is conse-
quent upon the reality of God in Christ, the 'essence of the
Church'; it is the 'possibility' that rests upon the presupposition that God in Christ approaches us in a uniquely
distinctive and irreducibile way.

What then does this fundamental datum of the 'essence of
the Church' consist in? It is not anything that the Church
possesses, just as it was not anything possessed by Bible or
tradition. It is, Barth argues, a 'pure act', an utterly original
(and, therefore, underived) divine action, which has its own

81

basis and is essentially self-explanatory. Knowledge of it is not speculative but an acknowledgment of a given which is independent of all human causation and truly autonomous. The occasion of this divine act is the Church's proclamation in which, in accordance with Reformation principles, the essential sacramental medium is the preached Word of God. God objectifies himself according to his own grace and will in his language, in a manner analogically parallel to Christ's own assumption of human flesh. As with Christ, so with the Word of God; the analogy is in fact an identity, for revelation is, has been and will be the Person of Jesus Christ. In asserting that revelation is, the statement is made and repeated that 'The Word became flesh and dwelt among us'.[7] This carries with it the inescapable implication that 'we are asserting something that is to be grounded only within the Trinity; namely, by the will of the Father, by the mission of the Son and of the Holy Spirit, by the eternal decree of the Triune God'.[8] Thus it is that revelation is an immediate implication of the Trinity itself. God is in his revelation; the implication is mutual and complementary for there is, according to Barth, no hidden abyssmal God apart from his revelation in Jesus Christ and correspondingly no revelation of God that does not express God in his fullness.

The mystery of God's uncreated reality in the Word is a veiling of God in which he unveils himself. This is the dialectic of the worldliness of the transcendent Word, that presents itself in an irresolvable tension demanding acknowledgment and resisting reductive explanation. The general principle of the worldliness of the Word incarnate, which has replaced the utter disjunction of divine and human existence, characteristic of dialectical theology as such, is supplemented by a further 'analogy' which provides the initial step in translating the argument from the doctrine of the Word to that of the Trinity, 'the doctrine of the three-in-oneness of God'. The doctrine of the Trinity has no analogy other than that of the threefold form of the Word of God (preached, written and revealed) and, the analysis of the concept of revelation yields the doctrine of the Trinity. The content of the 'original reality' or revelation is the 'analytical judgment' that 'God reveals Himself as Lord'. Revelation is not argued to, but is a self-grounded and self-authenticated fact, which occurs on the basis of God's sovereign freedom. From this 'fact' of the free lordship of God that happens in revelation there may take place the analytical (indeed it might be said tautologous) derivation of the truth that 'Godhead in the Bible means freedom, ontic and noetic independence'.[9]

Repudiating decisively the Augustinian attempt to isolate traces of the Trinity in the created world, because of his desire to safeguard completely the absolute primal uniqueness of the revelation of God, Barth proceeds towards what he conceives of as the legitimate 'interpretation' (as opposed to the 'illustration') of revelation. The only veridical trace of revelation is that of God's Word (not one expressed in the human psychology of memory, thought and will, for example) in which there is the triply one voice of Father, Son and Spirit speaking in his revelation, in Holy Scripture and in proclamation. This is the exclusive basis of our knowledge of the Trinity.

There is undoubtedly a profoundly rhapsodic quality to Barth's argument; the fundamental nature of revelation and thus God's own making accessible of himself makes it inevitable that the logical path from the realm of immanence to that of transcendence is incomplete precisely because of the nature of the subject in question. Once it has been made clear that God has in reality acted (and acts) in the way he did (and does) then the inner logic of his nature unfolds strictly upon its own terms, as an exegesis of the events of revelation witnessed to in Holy Scripture. For Barth it may then be said that the Trinity creates its own evidence and all other 'evidence' is of necessity misleading and perversely false.

The Trinity, as the 'possibility' lying behind the 'reality' of revelation, is now explicated in the context of the 'analytical' sphere of the trinitarian act of God in revelation, an act which supremely expresses the three-in-oneness. It is the point of derivation of the doctrine of the Trinity in the single (yet temporally extended and recurrent) act of God in revelation which dictates the fundamental commitment to the principle of unity in the trinitarian thought of the *Church Dogmatics*. Such a point of unity is also taken by many critics of Barth as an indication of an essential Christomonism in his scheme. The complete and comprehensive source of the knowledge of God in his revelation in Christ and the derivation of the dogmatic structure from this 'fact' has been seen as a principle which obscures and reduces the reality and importance of these other items on the christian theological agenda. The claim made by Barth is that the Trinity is not a merely formal explanation of revelation but its ontological enabling, the real possibility behind the revealed reality. This potential reductive criticism of Barth must be borne in mind as the explicit logic of the Trinity is unfolded, for it is possible that here is encountered a source not only of Barth's 'Christomonist' tendency but also of the heavy emphasis he places upon the unity of God's 'ways of being' in the Father, Son and Holy Spirit.

The exposition of the trinitarian being of God in Father, Son and Holy Spirit that Barth provides is in terms of three 'modes' or 'ways of being', which indicate a threefold repetition and mutuality that is so complete as to allow a complete 'involution' and 'convolution' of these 'modes' in a 'single act' of revelation, for all God's operation, as we are bound to conceive it on the basis of his revelation, is a single act, occurring simultaneously and unitedly in all his three modes of existence. Indeed, Barth argues, from 'creation, past revelation and reconciliation, to the redemption to come it holds good, that He who acts here is the Father and the Son and the Spirit'.[10] God is fully trinitarian but any such assertion is subordinated to the demands of singularity posited in the act of revelation, in which the eternal antecedence of God in Trinity is given temporal realisation in this 'single act'.

A certain tension in Barth's trinitarian thought is apparent at this point, for despite his reciprocal exposition of the oneness in threeness (indicated by a reference to Luther's exposition of the baptism of Jesus in which Father, Son and Holy Spirit participate) the emphasis upon unity is predominant. This predominance is apparent in the explicative motifs that have been encountered earlier, the threefold Word of God, for example, in which the analogy of the Trinity of God is this single recurrent principle. Now it is reinforced by the description of the manifestation of God in Trinity as Revealer, Revelation and Revealedness. In other words the distinctiveness of divine function upon which meaningful distinction-in-unity of the 'modes' (Barth shrinks from the word 'person' as implying an anthropomorphism) relies is subsumed into moments in the act of revelation. This is to some extent a reductive account in that one functional category becomes the medium both of unity and ostensibly of distinction also. Again it must be noted that it is the biblical witness to the 'veiling, unveiling and impartation of God' that gives 'cause to speak of a threefold otherness of the one God' in the first place.[11] The function of the Trinity is revelation; content of revelation is the disclosure of the Lordship of the one God.

The reciprocity and co-equality of God's 'ways of being' so heavily stressed by Barth is a dogmatic conception that finds its consummate expression in the assertion that the 'Church

doctrine of the Trinity is a self-enclosed circle'.[12] Here what
has been 'analytical judgment' becomes, as 'self-enclosed
circle', an explicit presentation of the celestial tautology that
tells us that the Revealer is God. The potential weakness of
this conception stems not only from the fact (Barth admits)
that such extreme reciprocity is not admitted by the New
Testament itself but also a further tendency of this trinitarian
act to encircle and absorb not only the 'moments' of God's
revelation as Father, Son and Holy Spirit[13] and the events of
the New Testament, but beyond this, the whole scheme of
creation, incarnation and reconciliation, that is, reality as a
whole.

> And this Lord can be our God. He can meet us and unite
> us to Himself, because He is God in these three modes of
> existence as Father, Son, and Spirit, because creation,
> reconciliation, redemption, the entire being, language,
> and action in which He wills to be our God, is grounded
> and typified in His own essence, in His Godness itself. As
> Father, Son, and Spirit God is, so to speak, ours in
> advance. (*CD* I/1, p. 440).

The grounding and typifying of such diverse realities in the
essence of God, in his 'Godness itself', is an indication that
the doctrine of the Trinity as the explication of the divine
'possibility' that underlies the 'reality' of revelation is no
mere abstraction but bound up intimately with the total logic
of Barth's presentation of reality as such in the *Church
Dogmatics*. It is not by a mere chance that this assertion of the
inclusiveness of the divine prototypicality is associated with a
radical denigration of our own existence, for it is 'held by
Him, and only by Him, over the abyss of non-existence'.[14]
Our existence, Barth continues, is 'real so far as He wills and
posits it a real existence'. This negative strain in Barth's

thought leads to an over-all ambiguity in the presentation of reality as we know it on the mundane level and raises problems that can only be hinted at here. In positive terms the prototypical potential of the trinitarian divine being is expressed initially in Barth's exposition of the Fatherhood of God. The importance of this exposition is that it provides, within the confines of Barth's trinitarian framework, the detailed theological rationale for the inclusion (albeit prototypically) of all truly real reality, both created and recreated. The prototypic potential of Barth's doctrine of God in Trinity is of an extent determined by the temporal structure and extension of the single act of the divine being in revelation. The temporal inclusion which correlates with the prototypical capacity of the divine being has consequences which are extremely far-reaching. The centrality of the act of revelation and its temporal extension provides the prototypical basis, through its eternal status, of the whole temporal order of reality.

The trinitarian explanation of the divine being is part and parcel of an over-all structure which dominates and conditions the explicit theology of the Trinity. Such a theme as that of the Fatherhood of God is not only an exposition of divine personhood in reciprocal relation but the theological link relating Trinity to creation in the sphere of prototypical antecedence. From God's own Fatherhood of Jesus Christ may be derived prototypically not only fatherhood in general but the fact of creation itself, 'it is again as this Eternal Father, and not in any other way, that he reveals himself as the Creator'.[15]

Unfortunately, just as the outward limits of the doctrine of the Trinity imply an inclusion of the totality of reality (and this is especially clear with regard to time and human nature as the human nature of Jesus Christ) so inwardly such an inclusion has a corresponding compression and implicit

categorial reduction. The derivation of creation and created-
ness from the equation of Creator and Father in the context
of the Trinity means that once more the latter does not
remain so much a mystery transcending human rationality
as an ontological battle-ground whose strife is muted by a
suppression of incompatibles. Effectively all the tensions of
the antithesis of created and uncreated being of immanence
and transcendence are translated into the area of the
doctrine of the Trinity, precisely because the act of revelation
is the direct correlate of the Trinity and vice versa. This act is
the dialectical interplay of divine being and worldly mask in
revelation. The absolute identity of act and Trinity, of three-
in-oneness, means that an ontological compression has to
take place and evidence of this is apparent in the implications
of the equation of Fatherhood and Creatorhood that Barth
presents.

In the first part of this brief outline of Barth's doctrine of
the Trinity the dangers of his method of grounding and
deriving this conception from the 'single act' of the divine
being have become apparent. In crude but not inaccurate
terms it may be said that Barth effectively inverts the
Hegelian doctrine of the Trinity.[16] Hegel resolves the Trinity
into the historical process, God dies in Christ, history moves
towards its spiritual and intellectual consummation. Barth,
in positing the contingent historical order upon the basis of
the putative contingency and historicity of God, attempts to
recreate the natural order but by doing so effects a resolution
and extinction of that order in the trinitarian abyss of the
divine being. This is the primary significance of Barth's
doctrine of the Trinity which is no mere theological excursion
of some originality but a structural reinterpretation of reality
as a whole *within* the confines of fundamental dogma.

II. THE TRINITY AND THE STRUCTURE
OF CHURCH DOGMATICS

It is only upon the basis of the realisation of the global ontological and epistemological role of Barth's doctrine of the Trinity as the ostensible explication of God's act of revelation that the student may proceed without misconceptions to examine the burgeoning theological ornamentation of his work. Thus the exposition of the trinitarian 'modes' as stated initially in the Niceno-Constantinopolitan Creed that Barth then proceeds to develop must be understood and appreciated with caution. Without such caution a gross mystification may well overcome the reader as he becomes gradually enmeshed in the implications of Barth's basic theological method whilst he conceives of himself as engaged in mere doctrinal analysis. It is consequently necessary to analyse Barth's thought on at least two levels. The first of these has involved a critical appreciation of some of the reasons for the basic monism, or trend towards unity in the doctrine of the Trinity in the *Church Dogmatics*, which stems primarily from the mode of its generation and derivation in the so-called single act of revelation. Given this analysis, the second level concerns the actual dogmatic outworking of the doctrine in the architectonic structures of the *Church Dogmatics*. The former may not ultimately be divorced from the latter level for they are methodologically interwoven. Exploration of the trinitarian development extending from the genetic revelatory core outwards in the doctrines of election, incarnation, christology, creation and reconciliation reveals progressively both the strength and underlying weakness of Barth's doctrine of the Trinity. With enormous energy the doctrine of the Trinity is propounded in all these contexts inasmuch as Father, Son and Holy Spirit manifest themselves, but the unity thus achieved is matched by the dispersal of the initial difficulties, much in the way that an air-conditioning system may also distribute a poisonous gas to all parts of a large building.

In the latter stages of the exposition of the doctrine of the Trinity found in volume I/1 Barth provides a first schematic statement of the three different modes or ways of being. Here the essential scriptural reference of the exposition comes to the fore and Barth finds and exploits ample evidence for the fundamental work of the trinitarian revelation of God as Lord, Yahweh and Kyrios, in Old and New Testaments respectively. In specific terms it is in the life, death and resurrection of Jesus Christ that God as Father, Creator, and free, holy God is revealed. God's own capacity for such a revelation depends upon his being what he is in revelation antecedently in himself. The events of the life of Jesus Christ are the *sole* medium of revelation and in virtue of the trinitarian capacity in antecedence and reciprocity the *completeness* of revelation of Father, Creator and Lord is guaranteed. The exclusiveness of revelation in Jesus Christ depends absolutely upon the fullest form of trinitarian inclusiveness. Revelation is the *Novum* (a really new unveiling of mystery) because, 'Jesus did not so much reproclaim the familiar word "Creator" and interpret it by the likewise unfamiliar name of Father, but he revealed the unfamiliar Father, his Father, and thereby, and first thereby and only thereby that and what the Creator is, and that He as such is our Father'.[17] The fullest unity and integration of the doctrine of the Trinity is essential, if the fullness of revelation in God's act in Jesus Christ is to be preserved, given that no evidence in the cosmos, human life or even Holy Scripture can be taken as the basis of trinitarian inference, apart from the peculiar mode of trinitarian deduction made possible by entry into the 'self-enclosed circle' of the doctrine of the Trinity, a circle that becomes a reality in Jesus of Nazareth, and in him alone, uniquely and exclusively. This reality is one of mutual and reciprocal reflection', for Barth argues, 'We cannot call God the Father, without the Son and the Spirit, and we cannot call the Son Saviour or the Spirit Comforter, without implying the Father in both cases'.[18]

The unity in trinity of the divine action is sustained by Barth's exploitation of traditional dogmatic conception of 'appropriation' and 'communion' which relate the modes of existence. There must be mutual interpenetration and communion without mutual extinction or reduction to a 'neutral, undifferentiated fourth'. God's being both inwardly and outwardly is a work, an act which is distinctively trinitarian and yet indivisible through the mutuality of attribution. Yet, despite the indivisibility and mutuality of appropriation the inner distinctions of the Trinity secure, Barth asserts, the peculiar and apposite nature of certain statements applicable to this or that mode of existence of the Trinity. God the Father, Son and Holy Spirit are what they are both in mutuality *and* distinctiveness. Whether Barth's reunification of the so-called immanent and economic doctrines of the Trinity (that is God in Trinity in himself and in revelation, respectively) can be sustained without some of the dangers alluded to in this short account is open to doubt. At this point not merely Barth's understanding of the Trinity is called into question, but the whole western tradition. Since Augustine this has relied upon a 'filioquist' and christologically conditioned extrapolation of the doctrine of the Trinity in terms of ecclesiology and spirituality which has tended towards disintegration of the over-all trinitarian framework.

This fragmentation can be seen in many contexts, especially in the history of the doctrine of the Church which has, in Catholic traditions, focused upon the christologically-dominated motif of the prolonged Christ, the extended incarnation as the basis of the Church and christian life, and in Protestant thought, upon God's death in the man Jesus Christ and subsequent to this act upon the Holy Spirit as the primal instrument in the historical perpetuation of Christ in the Church. The point of focus of piety has thus shifted uneasily from the primal unity of God to Christ, from Father to Son and even to Spirit. This unease is expressed in recent controversy because without an adequate doctrine of the Trinity, and awareness of the need for it, the orientation of christian worship and theological understanding alights upon one aspect and interprets the whole in the light of one mode.[19]

The difficulties in Barth's doctrine of the Trinity must not be allowed to obscure the fact that in the *Church Dogmatics* he draws this conception back into the realm of theological import and thereby he challenges an environment interpreted largely through the monocular anti-dogmatic and anti-trinitarian perspective of the practitioners of the historical-critical method. His treatment of the Trinity is grandiose, yet as has been seen genetically suspect, because of the mode of derivation dictated by the difficulties of generating any doctrine of revelation in the present age. Nevertheless despite these difficulties, which find expression in deep tensions, distortions and ambiguities throughout the *Church Dogmatics,* Barth forces the theologically-concerned reader to consider a basic question. Is there a God to whom the New Testament witnesses? Has he revealed himself in Jesus Christ and does he continue to reveal himself in the Church in concert with the Holy Spirit or are we, in the words of T. F. Torrance, left with a mere word-play, the unprofessional, arbitrary theological jottings of the primitive churches? For Barth, if God is, then he is God in Trinity and not otherwise. His arguments are imperfect and incomplete, but they are worthy of the most serious attention, because

Richard Roberts

without doubt they point the reader to absolutely fundamental questions and re-open a level of discussion gradually
excluded and subdued in the history of modern theology.
The painful dilemma that faces us is this: without the Trinity
we have no basis for the unity and continuity of Christianity
with the tradition of Israel and its monotheism and we
should revert to Judaism and dispense finally with the
divinity of Christ. With the doctrine of the Trinity in its
Barthian form the danger of an inward reduction into a
christological exclusivity is only held off by assertion. Clearly
the former is only acceptable if unconditional surrender is the
order of the day, and the latter must therefore be regarded as
provisionally important even as Barth would wish it to be.
Barth must be taken seriously because he recommences the
serious theological game; but he must be understood in order
to be surpassed.

University of Durham   RICHARD ROBERTS

NOTES

1. *Church Dogmatics* (Edinburgh, 1975) I.1, p. ix. In this paper reference
   will be made to the early translation (1936) by G. T. Thomson.
2. *The Christian Faith* (Edinburgh, 1928) pp. 738–751.
3. *CD* I.1, p. 301. The doctrine of the Trinity fundamentally distinguishes
   'the Christian doctrine of God as Christian'.
4. *The Epistle to the Romans* (London, 1933).
5. cf. T. F. Torrance *Karl Barth. The Development of his Early Theology*
   (London, 1962).
6. *CD* I.1. p. 11 (Bromiley). See also H. Bouillard, *The Knowledge of God*
   (London, 1969), for a critique of Barth's conception of the 'analogy of
   faith'.
7. John 1.14 is Barth's scriptural *Leitmotif* in the great early volumes of
   the *Church Dogmatics*.
8. *CD* I.1, p. 134.
9. *CD* I.1, p. 352.

10. *CD* I.I, p. 430.

11. *CD* I.I, p. 431.

12. *CD* I.I, p. 436.

13. *CD* I.I, p. 437.

14. *CD* I.I, p. 446.

15. *CD* I.I, p. 12.

16. Such as it is expounded in *The Lectures on the Philosophy of Religion*, in particular volume III, to which Barth refers in his article on Hegel in *Protestant Theology in the Nineteenth Century* (London, 1972), pp. 384–421.

17. *CD* I.I, p. 449.

18. *CD* I.I, p. 453.

19. Don Cupitt's desire to return to a religion indicated by Jesus, that is worship of the Father, is a plea for what might be termed a new Judaism. Such a move is fully congruent with the rejection of an inflated christologically-obsessed conception of Christianity, which reposes the fullness of divinity in Christ in such a way as to strain the interpretation of the New Testament and denigrate the doctrine of the Trinity, whose essential transcendent mystery should provide depth and stability to the triplicity of the traditional conception of the divine activity. See *The Myth of God Incarnate* (London, 1978), pp. 145–6.

CHAPTER SEVEN

Bernard Lonergan

Born in Canada in 1904, Bernard Lonergan became a Jesuit priest. After study in England and Rome he taught in Canada for thirteen years before becoming professor of theology at the Gregorian University in Rome. Since his retirement in 1965 he has lived and taught in North America. He is to be reckoned among the most important dogmatic theologians of this century and he has the rare distinction of having conferences devoted to the examination of his theology and philosophy.[1]

Instead of assuming that one or other contemporary philosophy or world-view is correct, Lonergan sets out to determine the structure of the human mind which has given rise to the variety of philosophies and world-views, and, on the basis of which each is to be criticised as inadequate. He goes on to apply this structure to the business of theology. In what follows, I shall attempt to outline his notion of theology in general, and his application of it to the doctrine of the Trinity.

I. THE APPROACH TO THEOLOGY

It is in many ways unfortunate that *Method in Theology* is so much better known than the Latin treatises *De Deo Trino*, *De Verbo Incarnato*, and *De Constitutione Christi*, in which so much of Lonergan's most serious first-order theological work is to be found. If this background is not taken into account, the very generalised approach of *Method in Theology* may appear irritating, and irrelevant to the immediate concerns of theologians. When Barth and Gogarten were in collaboration round about 1930, it has been said that the former would not face the question, 'When will you get your presuppositions clear?'; the latter, 'When will you get down to business?'.[2] A theologian who knew *Method* but not the Latin treatises might, in the event quite unfairly, press this latter question against Lonergan.[3]

Christianity is a faith to be proclaimed to all nations and cultures; yet as originally preached by Jesus and his disciples, it is very much in terms of its particular time and place. The development of doctrine is due partly to the need to translate what is expressed in terms of one cultural background into terms intelligible to another; it is hardly relevant to the concerns of a first-century Roman or Illyrian, let alone to a twentieth-century Eskimo or Malaysian, that the Messiah or the Son of David has come into the world. But it is partly due to another fact. Men vary not only in their cultural backgrounds, but in the extent of their intellectual development. The primitive mind thinks pictorially and symbolically; it lacks the capacity to reflect on its own processes, and is a stranger to the niceties of logic and scientific method. These begin to be possible when people follow the example of Socrates, and start looking for the exact definition of the terms that they are using. As a result of such reflection what was originally expressed in a dramatic and poetic way is progressively able to be stated in a more and more exact and rigorous manner, by use of the kind of technical terminology which is most familiar to us from the natural sciences.

It is a cardinal feature of Lonergan's position that it was

this last which was primarily at issue in the development of christian doctrine from New Testament times, through the deliberations of the Greek councils, and up to the era of the great Scholastics. Thus on his view it is completely wide of the mark to suggest, as is so often done, that what was going on was the 'corruption' of something 'dynamic' and 'Hebraic' into something 'static' and 'Greek', as though these qualities reverently attributed to Hebrew thought by some theologians were not everywhere characteristic of the primitive mind. Nor can the change be reversed, short of an obscurantist flight to the primitive which rejects most of the intellectual achievements of the last two thousand years in logic, philosophy and the sciences. The fact is that, to any mind which is in the least reflective, the New Testament when taken as a whole gives rise to a formidable collection of intellectual puzzles, the attempted solutions to which give us the series of heresies and the progress of orthodoxy. Who and what is this Jesus, who is apparently so closely associated with God? Is he just a man with a unique commission from God? Is he simply identical with God? If he was truly divine, was he only apparently human? Is he the highest and noblest and first-created of all creatures, but not strictly speaking divine? Or is he somehow at once really and truly the eternal divine Word of God the Father, and yet none the less a man who lived on earth at a particular time and place, with human thoughts and feelings and a human capacity for suffering?

In the course of clarifying their own position against those of the heretics, the Fathers took a step of the utmost importance. It is often said that they took over Hellenic concepts or Hellenic philosophy in their recasting of the Faith. So some of them did; thus Tertullian drew on Stoic materialism in his explanation of the relation of the Father to the Son, which he thought of as a kind of material continuity; and Origen made the same kind of use of neo-Platonic thought. But neither Stoicism nor neo-Platonism, not any other Greek philosophical system, was essentially involved in the terminological innovation introduced by the Council of Nicaea. What was involved was not Hellnic *concepts*, but a Hellenic *technique*: that of clarifying by a linguistic rule what can and what cannot be said on any subject. The term *homoousios* was not in fact current in philosophy before that time. It was used for describing things 'of the same stuff', as two desks might be made out of the same sort of wood, or two coins of the same metal; the Fathers took this term over and used it in a metaphorical sense. What this sense was may be understood by consideration of the Arian account of the nature of the Son which the use of the term was specifically designed to exclude. According to the Arians, the Son was strictly speaking a creature, and, as such, must have come into existence in time. To say that the Son is consubstantial or *homousios* with the Father is to say, on the contrary, that the Son is really and truly divine, just as the Father is; and as a logical consequence could not be a creature or have come into existence in time. It is to observe the rule, as was pointed out by Athanasius, that the same things are to be said of the Son as of the Father, except only that the Son is not the Father.

The terminological innovation introduced at Nicea was supposed merely to meet an emergency; but once the process had begun, it could not be halted. Once it had been settled that the Son is consubstantial with the Father, the question could not but arise whether the Holy Spirit also is so. It is to be noted that, on this account of the matter, what these early Councils imposed, and according to many still impose, on Christians, is not some abstruse metaphysical speculation of Hellenic origin, but a rule about what may or may not be said about Christ and the Holy Spirit in relation to what is said about God the Father. Just the same principles are to be applied to the interpretation of the Council of Chalcedon. Against Nestorius, Cyril of Alexandria had insisted that it was *one and the same* who was at once the eternal Word of God, and had been born of the Virgin Mary; it was not a question of *two beings* united however intimately together. On the other hand, this one being had two 'natures' in the plain sense that he was both really and truly divine, and really and truly human. To put it in more contemporary terms, what the conciliar formula amounted to is that there was one and the same individual ('person'), Jesus Christ, who had two sets of properties ('natures'), by virtue of one of which he was a man, by virtue of the other of which he was God. As in the case of Nicea, it is not helpful to look in contemporary or earlier philosophical writers to try to determine what the Fathers meant by 'person' or 'nature', at least until one has attended to the difficulties and disputes which they were trying to resolve. Certainly *hypostasis* (person) and *physis* (nature), unlike *homoousios*, were words which already had currency in philosophy as technical terms; but the Fathers used them in their own way and for their own purposes. Again, no abstruse metaphysical speculation is involved in the definition, whose effect is simply to insist that one and the same is both divine and human. It leaves one free to conceive of God and man in a vast range of ways, merely imposing the rule that, whatever it is to be God, Jesus Christ is to be held to be that; and whatever it is to be man, Jesus Christ is to be held to be that too.[4]

The early Councils used systematic devices and terminology to meet particular emergencies that arose. In the medieval period, particularly from the end of the eleventh century till the end of the thirteenth, the attempt was made to express the christian faith in systematic terms. Abelard's *Sic et Non* brought out vividly that on a whole range of issues

Scripture and the Fathers contradicted themselves and one another; given that the christian faith was founded upon these authorities, what was to be done? The great *Summae*, of which Aquinas's two masterpieces are the most well known, met the issue by lining up the contradictions, and tackling the problems that they revealed; the result was a systematic presentation of the christian faith, that is, one in which the meanings and inter-relations of its constituent propositions were precisely determined. The work of Aristotle commended itself as the best available framework on the basis of which this could be done.

The best of this achievement is to be understood not as a blasphemous replacement of faith by philosophical argument, but as 'faith seeking understanding', as a sustained and largely successful attempt to explain *why* and *how* those things were so which the Church proclaimed to be so, both through the relations of the revealed mysteries to one another, and through their significance for authentic human development and its consummation in the vision of God. However, by the fourteenth century scholasticism had declined, and theological advance was on the whole halted as a result. This was largely due to two defects in the work of Aristotle himself, which were to do equivalent though less long-term damage to the secular sciences when they emerged four centuries or so later. One of these defects was the conception of science as knowledge of the necessary; the other was an excessive emphasis on deductive logic in the business of establishing what is so. If science were really confined to knowledge of the strictly necessary, it would not be very useful for finding out about what goes on in a contingent world, or about the nature of its Creator's freely gracious activity in remedying the defects of such a world and bringing it to its full perfection. Now Aristotle, whatever the implications of the principles which he set out in the *Posterior*

Analytics, largely avoided these defects in his own writings; and Aquinas, while he accepted Aristotle's notion of science, adroitly side-stepped the *prima facie* implications for his own work by maintaining that theology could only be a science in the strict sense of the word in the minds of the blessed in heaven. Here below, on his account, one has to proceed by a method which turns out to be astonishingly similar to that of hypothesis, deduction and verification which is the hallmark of modern science. A coherent system of concepts is worked out, in the course of theological investigation, which may be verified by appeal to Scripture, the consensus of the Fathers, and conciliar decrees; and which is an explanation not of what is *absolutely necessary,* but of what *is as a matter of fact so* by the grace of God, in such a way that it can be defended against objections, and shown to be internally coherent. But from the fourteenth century onwards, the emphasis was on what could be logically deduced from revealed doctrines rather than on faith seeking understanding. And it is obvious enough that, except on a very inexact conception of the nature of 'logic', the doctrines of the Church cannot be logically deduced from statements in Scripture.[5]

In Lonergan's view, medieval systematic theology at its best stands to Scripture in just the same relation as the explanatory scheme of modern chemistry stands to all the observations and experiments in relation to which it can be tested, and by deference to which it has evolved. One might teach chemistry either by describing how the discoveries were made, and so how the system of contemporary chemistry actually came into being; or by starting with the system of contemporary chemistry, and showing how observations and experimental results come out in accordance with it. It is notable that Lonergan's two textbooks on the Trinity are composed in accordance with these two models. The *Pars Systematica* starts from the psychological analogy employed for the understanding of the Trinity by Augustine, Aquinas and Lonergan himself; demonstrates how the two processions yield four distinct real relations, and the four distinct real relations three Persons; and finally brings out how the missions of the second and third Persons are described in the New Testament. The *Pars Dogmatica* proceeds in the reverse order, starting with the New Testament, explaining the rationale behind each step in the formulation of the doctrine of the Trinity, and concluding with the psychological analogy by means of which it may in some sort be explained.

The main task of contemporary systematic theology, as Lonergan sees it, is to take further the positive side of the medieval achievement. What the Greek Councils inaugurated, and the medievals at their best achieved, was a recasting of christian doctrine in a manner appropriate to what may be termed the systematic 'differentiation of consciousness', and which enables its meaning to be fixed with sufficient precision to be transferable between different cultural backgrounds. The same 'differentiation of consciousness' has given rise, especially since the seventeenth century, to the tremendous achievement of the physical sciences. But contemporary theology has to take account of yet another 'differentiation of consciousness', the scholarly one which was the achievement of the nineteenth-century German historical school. It is this 'differentiation of consciousness' which enables the historian of one culture to recover the viewpoint of members of another culture, even one far removed from him in space and time. The coming into existence of this new 'differentiation of consciousness', and its applications to biblical studies, renders more acute than ever the difficulties resulting from the *prima facie* differences, on which the Protestant Reformers laid such stress, between what seemed to be revealed in Scripture on the one hand, and what the Church had defined in the course of the centuries on the other. Awareness of this problem ought to drive christian theologians to yet another 'differentiation of consciousness', that of 'interiority', whereby one may articulate those basic mental operations which are constitutive of common-sense consciousness, and of the systematic and historical differentiations of consciousness, and set out their relation to one another. In this way the systematic theologian may apprehend what unity in faith there may be over a succession of cultures and through a variety of formulations, without in any way going against, and indeed taking full advantage of, the findings of historians.[6]

II. THE TRINITY

The essence of Lonergan's theology of the Trinity is a transposition into terms of interiority of the classical doctrine worked out by the Fathers on the basis of Scripture and defined by the early Councils of the Church, and elaborated in fully systematic and metaphysical terms by the great Scholastics. One might put it that what the Scholastics expressed in terms of metaphysics is expressed by Lonergan in terms of psychology; 'three Persons in one Substance' becomes three subjects of a single consciousness. This is not, as he would see it, to replace the old doctrine with a new; but to explain the old doctrine in terms which take account of questions which have been raised and difficulties which have arisen since its original formulation.[7]

The object of theology on Lonergan's view, as has already been said, is not to *prove* the truths of revelation, let alone to *replace* them; it is rather to gain some *understanding*, within the limits possible to men on earth, of what one accepts by faith that God has revealed about himself. This makes it the more

possible to relate life in all its aspects to God. By sustained
reflection on the revelation contained in the New Testament,
it is to be learned that, while there is but one God, there are
three beings, distinct in virtue of their mutual relations, who
are God. This paradox may be understood, indirectly and
incompletely (since we do not enjoy a direct vision of God
along with the blessed in heaven) and yet very usefully,
through what is known as 'the psychological analogy'; that is
to say, on the model provided by human consciousness and
its acts. I may form a more or less adequate conception of
myself; and I may evince more or less love of myself as so
conceived. Similarly, one may suppose that God who is
unrestricted understanding eternally forms a conception or
'inner Word' of himself, and eternally evinces love of himself
as so conceived. Now my conception of myself may be more
or less in accordance with reality, my approval of myself as so
conceived more or less appropriate or inappropriate. But
God's conception of himself, since his knowledge is perfect
and unrestricted, cannot be less than wholly adequate; and
his love of himself in accordance with this conception cannot
be less than wholly appropriate and honourable. As understanding forming conception, God 'begets'; as conception or
'inner Word' formed by that understanding he is 'begotten';
as evincing love in accordance with this conception he
'spirates'; as love thus evinced he is 'spirated'. As begetting
God is Father; as begotten he is Son; as spirating he is Father
and Son together; as spirated he is Holy Spirit. So it is that
the two processions in God, of which we find an analogy in
human consciousness, yield four 'relations', and the four
'relations' three 'Persons'.[8]

Someone might object that even if one can show by the
psychological analogy that the doctrine of the Trinity need
not strictly speaking be a contradiction, its truth would be
completely irrelevant to the human situation. Thus it is

worth noting that, if the psychological analogy as presented by Lonergan is on the right lines, the Holy Trinity constitutes the ideal of our relations both to ourselves and to other persons. A human being's relationship to himself is typically vitiated by the fact he cannot love himself so far as he has an adequate conception of himself; so he forms a distorted conception of himself in order to protect his self-esteem. The same, *mutatis mutandis,* applies to our relationships with other persons and groups; we tend to misrepresent others because we hate or despise them, and to hate or despise them because we misrepresent them. To share in the life of the Trinity, as is brought out particularly by the Gospel and First Epistle of John, is to follow the way of truth and love.[9]

What is the relation between the processions and the missions of the Persons? Now the sending of the Son and the Spirit are contingent events taking place in space and time; and what takes place in space and time cannot change eternal relations between eternal Persons. There might have been no act of creation at all, no world, no man, no sin, and so no missions of the divine Persons into the world and to men to remedy the effects of sin. It may be concluded that the missions consist of the eternal processions together with certain contingent effects; this effect in the case of the mission of the Son consists in a human life lived by the eternal Word, in the case of the Spirit in a body of men being brought into a state of love with God. As a result of these missions, men, possessed by the Spirit in the fellowship of the Son, are purged from the effects of sin and brought to a state of supernatural perfection.[10]

In what sense, if any, it may be asked, does the New Testament provide the basis for the doctrine that there are three distinct beings who are God, and yet that there is one God, as implied by the doctrine of the Trinity? That Christ is in some sense other than the Father goes without saying; the whole New Testament clearly presupposes it. Those who complain that an explicit statement of Christ's divinity is so rare in the New Testament forget the fact that, where a startlingly new teaching is to be communicated, linguistic usage changes only gradually, since otherwise what is said is bound to be misunderstood. What later can be expressed plainly and even with technical precision, has at first to be put over indirectly, in terms of symbol and parable. And if Jesus had said directly to the Jews that he was God, this would have meant to them that he was none other than God the Father, which of course would have been heretical by later standards.[11]

In the New Testament it is notable that the First Person of the Trinity – to use the terminology which evolved much later – is sometimes referred to simply as 'God', sometimes simply as 'the Father'; as though hinting that another divine being is to be revealed, the Son. And there is a concomitant variation in the terms applied to Jesus. When the Father is referred to simply as 'God', Jesus is apt to be designated 'Son of God' or 'Son of Man'. Where there is talk of 'God the Father', Jesus is usually termed 'Son of the Father' or 'his Son'. Where God the Father is simply 'the Father', Jesus is simply 'the Son'. Thus in the Gospel of John Jesus is often called 'the Son' without addition or qualification, which is rare in the Synoptics (Mark 13.32; Matt. 11.27; 24.36; 28.19; Luke 10.22). Pauline usage is intermediate in this respect between the Synoptics and John.[12]

The divinity of the Son is suggested or implied by the New Testament in many places. Jesus speaks with the authority of God;[13] unique knowledge of the Father is claimed for him (Matt. 11.27; Luke 10.22); the prophetic 'day of the Lord' becomes the day of Jesus Christ (1 Cor. 1.8; 5.2; 2 Cor. 1.14; 1 Thess. 5.2; 2 Thess. 2.1–2; 2 Pet. 3.10); preparation of the way of the Lord (Mal. 3.1) is the preparation of the way of

Christ (Mark 1.3); the Son is the equal of the Father (John 5.17–27), and to know the Son is to know the Father (John 14.7–11); he is associated with the Father in the work of creation (1 Cor. 8.6; Col. 1.16; Heb. 1.2–3; John 1.3); all that belongs to the Father belongs to the Son (John 16.15; 17.10); the Son as well as the Father is worthy of the titles 'Alpha and Omega', 'beginning and end', 'first and last' (Rev. 1.8, 17; 2.8; 21.6; 22.13); and he is 'the Word' who was with the Father in the beginning (John 1.1). Of course, the texts which do directly maintain the Son's divinity (2 Pet. 1.1; Titus 2.13; Heb. 1.9; John 20.28; 1 John 5.20) should not be left entirely out of account; though it would be a complete misunderstanding on Lonergan's view to regard them as the sole or the chief basis in Scripture for christian belief in the divinity of Christ.[14] And once the divinity of the Son is established, the way is open to belief in the divinity of the Spirit who is so often associated with the Father and the Son in the epistles and John's Gospel.

Lonergan's account of the Trinity illustrates his general position on the relation of philosophy to systematic theology.[15] Systematic theology, presupposing as it does the acceptance of a revelation on faith, cannot be *reduced* to philosophy; on the other hand, the two ought to exist in close and fruitful collaboration. Lonergan does believe, in common with the generality of Roman Catholic theologians, that the existence of God can be established by rational argument, though he thinks that such arguments are very seldom means to conversion; but he does not think that one can possibly establish the existence of the Trinity as such in this kind of way. But this by no means implies that philosophy is of no use for speculation on the Trinity. A distinction is to be made between practical and existential consciousness. I am practically conscious in thinking out a course of action, like making a bed or writing a theological article, and

Bernard Lonergan

putting it into effect; I am existentially conscious in forming a conception of and taking up an attitude to myself. God can be shown to exist as practically conscious, as an intelligence who conceives and puts into effect states of affairs, through a consideration of the nature and structure of the universe;[16] but he cannot be thus shown to be existentially conscious. On the other hand, he cannot be thus shown to be *not* existentially conscious; and the supposition that he is so makes sense of divine revelation as originally given in the New Testament and as expounded over the course of the centuries by the Church.

Lonergan's theology of the Trinity is a compelling intellectual achievement; but it stands or falls as providing a glimpse 'through a glass darkly' of the glorious mystery of mysteries, the triune God revealed in our Lord Jesus Christ. I remain to be convinced that those modern theologians who purport to have got beyond the doctrine of the Trinity, at least as traditionally understood, have either Lonergan's intellectual power, or his insight into Scripture, the Christian tradition, and the real bearing of modern culture on the faith of the Church.

University of Leeds   HUGO MEYNELL

NOTES

1. See, e.g., the three volumes of papers given at the International Lonergan Congress of 1970, edited by Philip McShane, SJ.
2. Cf. E. Busch, *Karl Barth. His Life and Letters and Autobiographical Texts* (London, 1976), p. 194.
3. The main works which are relevant for a consideration of Lonergan's account of the Trinity are: *De Deo Trino*. I. *Pars Dogmatica*. II. *Pars Systematica* (Rome, 1964); *Verbum. Word and Idea in Aquinas* (London,

1968); and *Method in Theology* (London, 1971), especially the second paragraph of page 291, and chapters 12 and 13. *De Verbo Incarnato* (Rome, 1964) will also be referred to. These works will be designated respectively as *DDT* I, *DDD* II, *VWIA*, *MT* and *DIV*, in the following notes.

4. For these paragraphs, cf. especially 'The Dehellenization of Dogma' in *A Second Collection* (London, 1974), pp. 11–32, in which is to be found Lonergan's clearest and most readable brief account of his view of the achievement of the Greek Councils. Cf. also *The Way to Nicea* (London, 1976), a translation of part of *DDT* I.

5. Cf. *MT*, pp. 279–81, 297.

6. On 'differentiations of consciousness', cf. *MT*, pp. 258–62, 302–19. Lonergan distinguishes some others, which it has not seemed relevant to go into here.

7. Cf. 'The Dehellenization of Dogma', p. 25; *DDT* II, *passim*. Similarly, the systematic problems of christology are to be resolved on the basic postulate of 'a single subject of both a divine and a human consciousness', 'The Dehellenization . . .', *loc. cit.*; and *De Constitutione Christi* (Rome, 1956), *passim*.

8. Cf. *VWIA*, ch. 5; *DDT* II, chs. 2–5. Of great importance here is the principle enunciated by the Council of Florence (1438–9), that in God all is one where a mutual opposition of relations is not involved. Cf. *DDT* II, pp. 80, 127.

9. Lonergan argues in fact that some basis in Scripture for the psychological analogy is to be found in John's Gospel and First Epistle; cf. *DDT* I, pp. 279–98. A positivist or behaviourist might protest that he was never aware of engaging in the mental activities on which Lonergan founds the pyschological analogy. This would imply that he was never aware of saying anything for sufficient reason, and never did anything because he approved of it as suitable and honourable. Such an admission would seem to be somewhat damaging, not to say self-destructive. Cf. *MT*, pp. 16–17; *DDT* I, pp. 278–9. On the effect of the missions on human relations, cf. *DDT* I, 243–53.

10. *DDT* II, ch. 6.

11. *DVI*, pp. 23, 50.

12. *DDT* I, p. 124.

13. This is particularly emphasised by many of the proponents of the 'new quest for the historical Jesus'; cf. W. Pannenberg, *Jesus, God and Man* (London, 1968), pp. 53–66.

14. *DDT* I, pp. 125–7; *DVI*, pp. 43–5, 61, 83–4, 91, 93.

15. On this point, cf. especially *Philosophy of God and Theology* (London, 1973).
16. *DDT* II, pp. 105–6. Lonergan's argument for the existence of God is elaborated in *Insight. A Study of Human Understanding* (London, 1957), ch. 19. Cf. also *A Second Collection*, pp. 90–92, 117–33.

CHAPTER EIGHT

Jürgen Moltmann

Jürgen Moltmann, professor of systematic theology in the University of Tübingen, is currently working on a study of the doctrine of the Trinity. This chapter can therefore be no more than an interim report, tracing the development of Moltmann's thinking about the Trinity in his published work so far, and indicating aspects which we may hope will be clarified and developed in his forthcoming work.

I. ESCHATOLOGY

Moltmann's early work contains little explicit reference to the Trinity, although a doctrine of the Trinity is everywhere presupposed. The key position to which Barth assigned the doctrine of the Trinity is occupied in Moltmann's *Theology of Hope* by eschatology. It is eschatology which provides the interpretative category for understanding the Christ event:

> 'The eschatological is not one element *of* Christianity, but it is the medium of Christian faith as such, the key in which everything in it is set. . . . There is therefore only one real problem in Christian theology . . . : the problem of the future. . . . The God spoken of here is not intra-worldly or extra-worldly God, but the "God of hope" (Rom. 15.13), a God with "future as his essential nature" (as E. Bloch puts it), as made known in Exodus and in Israelite prophecy, the God whom we therefore cannot really have in us or over us but always only before us, who encounters us in his

promises for the future, and whom we therefore cannot "have" either, but can only await in active hope. A proper theology would therefore have to be constructed in the light of its future goal. Eschatology should not be its end, but its beginning.' (*TH* p. 16)[1]

Thus not the doctrine of the Trinity as analysis of the concept of revelation, but eschatology as the future orientation of all theological concepts, must stand at the beginning of systematic theology.

Moltmann's criticism of Barth on this point emerges in his discussion of the concept of revelation (*TH* ch. 1). Moltmann proposes an eschatological understanding of revelation as promise. Revelation is not the epiphany of an eternal, nontemporal truth. God does not make himself known to man in a moment of non-temporal present, without history or future. For Moltmann such a notion of revelation always derives ultimately from a Greek understanding of temporality, according to which truth cannot be found in the movement of history but only in an absolute present which has no extension in time. The biblical God, by contrast, makes himself known in his promises for the temporal future, whereby history acquires direction and meaning. What is promised is no mere unveiling of what is already true, but rather a new, not yet existing reality. The revelation of God's divinity entirely depends on the fulfilment of this promise for the transformation of reality. Thus the question of the provability of God with which modern discussion of the doctrine of revelation is obsessed can be answered only in hope for the promised future of God.

In this context Moltmann criticises Barth's understanding of the self-revelation of God in relation to the immanent Trinity. In so far as Barth's concept means that God reveals himself by taking man into the circle of his own eternal self-knowledge, it is a version of the 'epiphany of the eternal present'. Here Barth is still affected by the Platonic thinking of his dialectical phase. It is true, of course, that Barth's concept of the self-revelation of God is intended to refer to the history of Jesus Christ, but Moltmann finds it inappropriate for that purpose. The event of the resurrection of Christ cannot be understood as 'the pure presence of God', 'a present without any future'; it must on the contrary be understood as an event of promise which points beyond itself to the not yet existing reality of the future (*TH* pp. 50–58). Moltmann here sees his work as continuing the direction of the greater emphasis on the temporal future in Barth's own later work (*TH* p. 87).

Moltmann's fundamental criticism of Barth's doctrine of the immanent Trinity, then, is that it makes the history of Jesus Christ a revelation of eternity instead of a revelation of the future. This is not a rejection of the doctrine of the Trinity as such, but an argument for a version of that doctrine which takes more seriously the historical and eschatological character of the economic Trinity. Moltmann's theology cannot do without a doctrine of the Trinity, since the eschatology which controls it is founded on the cross and resurrection of Christ and is in process through the work of the Spirit. But the trinitarian truth of God is not given as the disclosure of supra-temporal truth; it is the truth of Jesus Christ who still awaits his future, of the Spirit which is the power of the resurrection of the dead, and of God who still waits to be 'all in all'. Already in *Theology of Hope* Moltmann presupposes, without developing, a concept of the Trinity as process open to the still outstanding future of God.

For Moltmann the danger of a doctrine of the immanent Trinity will be its tendency to obscure the eschatological direction of the economic Trinity (cf. *TH* p. 57). A doctrine of the immanent Trinity seems necessary in order to guarantee

that the economic Trinity is God as he really is in himself
(*TH* p. 56), but it must not be allowed to reduce God's
activity in time to a disclosure of his eternal being.
Moltmann's thought seems to demand the recognition of an
element of genuine temporal becoming in God, since only
this will guarantee the biblical perception that truth is to be
found in event, in history and eschatology, rather than in the
eternal being of the Greeks which empties the temporal
process of significance. This seems to require that instead of
simply an immanent Trinity non-temporally 'behind' the
economic Trinity, we shall need to think of both a trinitarian
origin and a trinitarian goal of God's economic activity.

Just such a concept we shall see that Moltmann develops
in his latest work. That he was already thinking on these lines
soon after the publication of *Theology of Hope* is clear from a
letter he wrote to Karl Barth in April 1965. Barth had written
to him about *Theology of Hope*, criticising its onesided
emphasis on the futurity of God and suggesting that if
Moltmann had retained Barth's doctrine of the immanent
Trinity his concept of God would have been richer.
Moltmann's reply confessed that this point in Barth's
criticism caused him 'the worst headache'. It is New
Testament exegesis which obliges him to think of the
lordship of Christ first of all in eschatological terms. For that
reason, he set out 'the doctrine of the economy of the Trinity
in such a way that it remains also open in front, and then
equally behind, towards an immanent Trinity'.[2] The issue of
what it means for the concept of God to acknowledge a
history and a future of God will remain a key question in
Moltmann's subsequent reflection of the Trinity.

II. THE CRUCIFIED CHRIST

In the period between *Theology of Hope* and *The Crucified God*

Moltmann's theology moved from a concentration on the significance of the resurrection of Christ to a concentration on the significance of the cross of Christ. This is a shift of emphasis only, since the whole of Moltmann's theology is rooted in the dialectic of cross and resurrection. The significance of the resurrection is found precisely in the fact that it is the resurrection of the *crucified* Christ, and similarly the cross must be understood as the cross of the *risen* Christ.

The shift of emphasis means that whereas in *Theology of Hope* it is the character of the *resurrection* of Christ as promise which raises a question about the doctrine of the Trinity, in *The Crucified God* it is the significance of the *cross* for the doctrine of the Trinity which Moltmann explores in some detail. The question of the trinitarian nature of God is raised more explicitly by the cross than by the resurrection.

This already becomes clear in lectures which Moltmann gave in 1968,[3] where he raises the christological question of Jesus' identity with God. This will be differently understood according as it is approached from the perspective of the resurrection or from the perspective of the cross. From the perspective of Jesus' resurrection as the anticipation of the eschatological future results a functional, adoptionist christology. In the resurrection, God, who has future as the mode of his being (*FH* p. 10), 'identifies himself with Jesus by receiving the crucified one into his future as mode of his being. If we start with the resurrection, we must say that God in his being does not become identical with Jesus, but identifies with Jesus through an act of his will' (*FH* p. 24). Jesus thus becomes God's deputy or 'stand-in', who in the period between his resurrection and ours, reigns over the world to subject it to God. He serves the limited function of preparing the way for God's complete kingdom.

This eschatological christology, however, misses the significance of the cross. The future of God's kingdom is not only anticipated in Jesus' resurrection, it is mediated to sinners by his cross. But the cross is not only, like the resurrection, God's act on Jesus. Not only did God offer up Jesus, 'but Jesus has also offered up himself and is one with the Father in his self-giving'. The Father's love takes the form of the obedience of his Son. 'In the obedience of the Son, therefore, we find the true image of God and not only a mediation that would become superfluous. The trinitarian relationship of the Father to the Son becomes the permanent characteristic of God. It is the inner rationale of God's reign' (*FH* p. 27). Thus God's future is not only anticipated in Christ; as the Son of the Father he is already the incarnation of the coming God (*RRF* p. 214, cf. *FH* p. 27) who mediates God's future to sinners as the fatherly love of God. The final handing over of the Kingdom to the Father will be the consummation of the Son's obedience, not the end of his sonship (*FH* p. 28, cf. *CG* pp. 264f.).

Moltmann here seems to be arguing that the relation of Jesus to God must be understood as a relationship within the being of God because this relationship is the form which God's love for sinners takes. Jesus is no mere dispensable deputy for God because his very being as the Son of his Father is the form of God's love for sinners. This way of thinking of the Incarnation enables Moltmann to conceive the unity of Father and Son in terms of will rather than substance: Jesus 'is one with the Father in his self-giving' (*FH* p. 27). It also suggests that at this stage Moltmann thinks of God as *becoming* Trinity in the history of Jesus: 'The trinitarian relationship of the Father to the Son becomes the permanent characteristic of God' (*FH* p. 27). This way of speaking Moltmann avoids in later work, but it results again from the problem of the temporality of God. Moltmann very much wished to understand the trinitarian relationship of Father and Son as a relationship which *happens* in the history of Jesus, and especially in the cross, and will not allow this happening to be a mere reflection of supra-temporal truth.

In these lectures of 1968, then, Moltmann argues that it is the significance of the *cross* of the risen Christ which requires expression in the trinitarian language of the relation of Father and Son. It also, he finds, requires expression in patripassian language: 'In Jesus' cross and resurrection God not only acts as Lord, but also suffers as Father in offering up his Son' (*FH* p. 28). These themes underwent considerable development in *The Crucified God*.[4]

III. THE CROSS AND THE CONCEPT OF GOD

The significance of the cross for the concept of God is such, according to Moltmann, as to call for a 'revolution in the concept of God' (*CG* p. 152). This radical significance depends on recognising the event of the cross as an event between God and God, between the Father and the Son, in which Jesus suffered abandonment by his Father. Moltmann considers the words 'My God, why hast thou forsaken me?' to be an early interpretation, but an accurate interpretation, of Jesus' dying cry (*CG* pp. 146f). Abandoned by the God whose closeness as his Father Jesus had known and whose identification with him Jesus had claimed in his ministry, Jesus on the cross sees his whole proclamation of God at stake. In his rejection the deity and the faithfulness of the God whom Jesus called Father is at stake (*CG* pp. 150f), and while God vindicated Jesus and confirmed his faithfulness in raising Jesus from the dead, it is still necessary – or rather it is therefore necessary – to understand God's activity in Jesus' passion. Here Moltmann's concept of the 'total contradiction' of cross and resurrection (*TH* p. 199), the contradiction of the godforsakenness of the crucified Jesus and the nearness of God in the raising of Jesus, from which

Jürgen Moltmann

Moltmann's whole theology developed, is restated in terms which demand a 'revolution in the concept of God': 'The cross of the Son divides God from God to the utmost degree of enmity and distinction. The resurrection of the Son abandoned by God unites God with God in the most intimate fellowship. How is this Easter day fellowship of God with God to be conceived in the Good Friday cross?' (*CG* p. 152).

'The death of Jesus is a statement about God himself' (*CG* p. 202): Moltmann attempts to work out consistently this observation of Karl Rahner. If God reveals himself in the godforsakenness of Jesus on the cross, then all other concepts of God must be given up and the attempt be made to understand the Christian God completely from the event of the cross (*CG* p. 190). This attempt soon finds it necessary to conceive God as Trinity, for: 'The cross stands at the heart of the trinitarian being of God; it divides and conjoins the persons in their relationships to each other and portrays them in a specific way' (*CG* p. 207). The death of Jesus is then to be understood not simply as the 'death of God' (the expression which Moltmann himself earlier used: *TH* pp. 168–72), but as 'death *in* God', an event within the relationship of the three persons, from which the meaning of Godhead emerges (*CG* p. 207).

If it is the event of the cross which requires trinitarian language, then the doctrine of the Trinity is no mere theological speculation remote from salvation-history, 'a kind of higher theological mathematics for the initiated' (*Theol* p. 632). If the relationships within the being of God are found in the event of the cross, then they are found within our human reality. The trinitarian nature of God is not a divine nature remote from man, but the human history of Jesus Christ (*CG* p. 239). Moltmann's formula for the relation between the theology of the cross and the doctrine of the Trinity makes each necessary to the other: 'The material

118

principle of the doctrine of the Trinity is the cross of Christ. The formal principle of knowledge of the cross is the doctrine of the Trinity' (*CG* p. 241).

What, then, is the event of the cross understood as an event between the persons of the Trinity? It is the event of God's love in which the Father forsakes his Son and delivers him to death so that the godless may not be godforsaken. The surrender of the Son to death is the action of both the Father and the Son, and in the suffering of the Son both Father and Son suffer, though in different ways. The Son suffers the abandonment by the Father as he dies; the Father suffers in grief the death of the Son. 'The grief of the Father here is just as important as the death of the Son' (*CG* p. 243).

Thus, in the cross, the Father and the Son are united in separation. Their unity is their 'deep community of will', in that the Son willingly surrenders himself to death, but this community of will 'is now expressed precisely at the point of their deepest separation, in the godforsaken and accursed death of Jesus on the cross' (*CG* pp. 243f). The cross is the salvific event of God's love because in it the love between the Father and the Son spans the gulf which separates godforsaken sinners from God. The trinitarian being of God includes this gulf within itself and thereby reaches sinners.

The powerful love which proceeds from this event between the Father and the Son is the Holy Spirit: the Spirit 'which justifies the godless, fills the forsaken with love and even brings the dead alive' (*CG* p. 244). The Spirit is 'the creative love proceeding out of the Father's pain and the Son's self-surrender and coming to forsaken human beings in order to open to them a future for life' (*Int* pp. 294f).

Thus the cross is the event in which God's love happens. 'God *is* love' means that God 'exists in love', that 'he constitutes his existence in the event of his love. He exists as love in the event of the cross' (*CG* p. 244).

At this point it is relevant that Moltmann in *The Crucified God*, following Rahner, has rejected the distinction between immanent and economic Trinity (*CG* pp. 239f). Thus the event of the cross is not the economic activity of the immanent Trinity; the event of the cross *is* the Trinity. Moltmann has also rejected the theological priority of his unity to his threefoldness (*CG* p. 239): the unity of God is found in the relation of the three persons. Thus the trinitarian God *is* the event of the cross. The trinitarian relationship of distinction in unity happens in the event of the cross. That event-character or historically of God's being which Barth finds in the event of God's self-revelation *and therefore* (because God corresponds to himself) *in the immanent Trinity*, Moltmann locates simply in the event of Christ itself:

'God's being is historical and . . . God exists in this specific history of Jesus Christ. . . . The word 'God' means an event, precisely this event. . . . Anyone who intends to speak in a Christian way about God must recount and proclaim this story of Christ as the story of God, that is, as something which occurred between Father, Son, and Spirit, and out of which the concept 'God' is constituted, not only for men but also for God himself. (*Int* pp. 294–6, cf. *CG* p. 247, *Conc* p. 35).

This claim that the event of the cross actually makes God who he is is an attempt to take absolutely seriously the idea of God's history, that God's involvement in the temporal experience of human history is real experience for God. If 'God' is the word for the trinitarian relationship of the three persons and if the human history of Jesus Christ is a real experience of trinitarian relationship for the three persons, then 'God' cannot be said to be who he is independently of this history. His temporal experience must make him who he is as human temporal experience makes human persons who they are.

Yet this would be a difficult idea to develop, in the extreme form which Moltmann here suggests, and it is significant that Moltmann has not developed it. His later work (so far published since *The Crucified God*) makes no reference to the event of the cross as *constituting* God's being, while in a passage in *The Church in the Power of the Spirit* which repeats Moltmann's trinitarian understanding of the cross, he says that in this event God is 'revealed' (not constituted) as the trinitarian God (*CPS* p. 96). This seems a significant retreat from the suggestions made in *The Crucified God*.

One possible interpretation of Moltmann's concept of the cross in *The Crucified God* might be that it is in the Christ event that God *becomes* Trinity, as we saw suggested in a 1968 lecture. Moltmann does not explicitly say this in *The Crucified God*, but it is not inconsistent with what he says. In *The Church in the Power of the Spirit*, as we shall see, he denies it and reverts to a doctrine of an immanent Trinity original to God prior to his 'history'. Whether the trinitarian being of God from eternity could be said to be constituted by the temporal event of the cross Moltmann does not enquire. The bold thesis of *The Crucified God* is left disappointingly unexplored in Moltmann's work to date, and even, it seems retracted in his latest work.

IV. THE SUFFERING GOD

Two further, interrelated, aspects of Moltmann's trinitarian thought in *The Crucified God* remain to be mentioned. The first is its relationship to the problem of suffering and theodicy which is a major concern of all Moltmann's work, and especially of *The Crucified God*.

Here Moltmann develops the claim that the specifically

Christian concept of God which develops from the cross is to be sharply differentiated from metaphysical theism, i.e. the philosophical concept of God which Christian theology largely took over in the patristic age. Theism defines God's infinity over against man's finiteness: the indivisible, immutable, immortal, omnipotent, impassible God is projected as a form of security for finite, mortal, weak, suffering, threatened man. But this concept of God as incapable of suffering must 'evacuate' the cross of deity (*CG* p. 214; cf. already *TH* p. 140). Moreover, the God who cannot suffer is poorer than man, for if he cannot be affected he cannot love (*CG* pp. 222, 253). The God of theism cannot be the God who in the suffering of the cross is 'love with all his being' (*CG* p. 205). Thus the cross must not be interpreted in the light of the theistic concept of God; it must on the contrary be a criticism of and liberation from theism (*CG* p. 216):

> With the Christian message of the cross of Christ, something new and strange has entered the metaphysical world. For this faith must understand the deity of God from the event of the suffering and death of the Son of God and thus bring about a fundamental change in the orders of being of metaphysical thought and the value tables of religious feeling. It must think of the suffering of Christ as the power of God and the death of Christ as God's potentiality. (*CG* p. 215)

God is not, like creatures, *subject* to change and suffering, but he is free to open himself to change and suffering out of the fullness of his being, which is love (*CG* pp. 229f, *CPS* p. 62).

A trinitarian theology of the cross, Moltmann claims, offers a way forward beyond the unsatisfactoriness of both theism and atheism in the face of the problem of suffering. Metaphysical theism infers its God from the world. Metaphysical atheism similarly infers the non-existence of God from the world. While theism sees the world grounded in the power and wisdom of a supreme being, atheism cannot believe that a good God can be responsible for a world in which evil and suffering are triumphant. But while theism cannot explain suffering without justifying it, nor can atheism eliminate the longing for God's righteousness in the world. No approach to the problem of suffering can be adequate which does not keep alive the protest against suffering and the longing for righteousness (*CG* pp. 219–226).

In Moltmann's trinitarian theology of the cross, however, God is no longer seen as an invulnerable divine being over against the suffering of the world. God himself suffers and in the dying question of the crucified Jesus he himself takes up humanity's protest against suffering and the open question of God's righteousness in the world (*CG* pp. 225–7). Thus for the sufferer God is not just the incomprehensible God who inflicts suffering, 'but in a profound sense the human God, who cries with him and intercedes for him with his cross where man in his torment is dumb' (*GC* p. 252). The question of God's righteousness in a suffering world is not suppressed but kept open by God himself in hope for the new creation of all things.

Moltmann's earlier explorations of theodicy stressed the *resurrection* of the crucified Christ as God's contradiction of evil, suffering and death, promising a corresponding new creation all reality (*TH* p. 21). This perspective is not superseded in *The Crucified God*, but Moltmann deepens it by stressing God's identification in the crucified Christ with all the suffering protest of humanity. In the trinitarian event of the cross all suffering is taken within the being of God and may thereby hope for participation in the joy of God's future. 'Like the cross of Christ, even Auschwitz is in God himself. Even Auschwitz is taken up into the grief of the Father, the surrender of the Son and the power of the Spirit' (*CG* p. 278).

This leads immediately to the second aspect of Moltmann's trinitarian thought in *The Crucified God*: that the event of the cross is not a finished event but initiates a trinitarian 'history' of God which is open to the eschatological future. The trinitarian relationship of God will itself be consummated only when the history of God's liberating love in the world, the history of the Spirit, is complete, when the Son hands over the Kingdom to the Father (1 Cor. 15.24), thereby consummating the obedient sonship of the Son and the fatherhood of the Father and the brotherhood of believers (*CG* pp. 265f).

What happened in the abandonment of Jesus on the cross was that the trinitarian being of God opened to include within itself the whole of human history in its godforsakenness and curse:

> All human history, however much it may be determined by guilt and death, is taken up into this 'history of God', i.e. into the Trinity, and integrated into the future of the 'history of God'. There is no suffering which in this history of God is not God's suffering; no death which has not been God's death in the history on Golgotha. Therefore there is no life, no fortune and no joy which have not been integrated by his history into eternal life, the eternal joy of God. (*CG* p. 246)

Thus for Moltmann the doctrine of the Trinity points to an eschatological 'panentheism': God has taken within himself all history, including the negative element in the world, so that he may overcome the negative and become 'all in all' (*CG* p. 277).

V. RESURRECTION AND THE SPIRIT

Douglas Meeks observes that the development of Moltmann's theology corresponds to the three trinitarian 'moments' of resurrection, cross and Pentecost (*EH* p. xi). The God of *Theology of Hope* is predominantly the God who raised Jesus from the dead, the God of hope, the eschatological God who has future as the mode of his being. The doctrine of the Trinity acquires much greater attention in *The Crucified God*, because here God is predominantly the incarnate God, the God who suffers and protests alongside suffering and godforsaken man, then God who takes all humanity within his suffering love. The eschatological perspective is far from being lost, but God himself is more deeply involved in the movement of history towards the future. Humanity as much as future is the mode of his being. He is not only out ahead of his people leading them forward to the promised land; he is also incarnate amongst them identified with their sufferings. In his third major work, *The Church in the Power of the Spirit*, Moltmann takes up the third trinitarian moment, Pentecost, and sees the Church within the trinitarian history of God initiated by the Christ event, and the Spirit as the power of God's trinitarian love moving history towards the eschatological Kingdom. In this context Moltmann is able to return to some of the themes of *Theology of Hope* – the mission of the Church and the eschatological goal of history – but to see them in the newly gained perspective of God's trinitarian history. The future of God is re-defined in trinitarian terms.

The trinitarian doctrine of *The Church in the Power of the Spirit* is set out succinctly in the section 'The Church in the Trinitarian History of God' (pp. 50–65).[5] Here Moltmann at last takes up the idea conveyed in the letter to Barth in 1965 that he wished to see the economic Trinity as open both in front and behind towards an immanent Trinity. At no previous point in his published work has Moltmann spoken of an immanent Trinity behind the economic Trinity, while the identification of immanent and economic Trinity in *The*

Crucified God seemed rather to eliminate such a concept. Now, however, Moltmann allows the validity of the traditional and Barthian inference back from the immanent Trinity to an immanent Trinity, which he prefers, however, to call the 'Trinity in the origin'.

The trinitarian history of God is grounded in the missions of the Son and the Spirit. But theological reflection must enquire about the origin of these missions, and following the principle that God corresponds to himself, must conclude that these economic relationships between the persons correspond to relations in eternity. The missions *ad extra* reveal missions *ad intra*: the eternal generation of the Son by the Father, and the eternal procession of the Spirit from the Father (or 'from the Father and the Son': Moltmann refuses to adjudicate the *filioque* issue). Only this inference from the 'Trinity in the sending' (as Moltmann now calls the economic Trinity) to the 'Trinity in the origin' can ensure that in the history of Jesus and the experience of the Spirit we have to do with God himself.

The inference, however, also has a second function: it shows the Trinity to have been from eternity an 'open Trinity. It is open for its own sending. . . . It is open for men and for all creation. The life of God within the Trinity cannot be conceived of as a closed circle – the symbol of perfection and self-sufficiency. . . . The triune God is the God who is open to man, open to the world and open to time' (*CPS* pp. 55f).

This protest against the 'closed circle' image of the Trinity already appeared in *The Crucified God* (pp. 249, 255), where the immanent Trinity as 'a closed circle of perfect being in heaven' was contrasted with the Trinity as the human historical event of Jesus Christ. Now, however, Moltmann admits the validity of the inference to an immanent Trinity 'in heaven' (i.e. in God's eternity without the world), insisting only that this Trinity be conceived as 'open' to the world. In this conception we should notice not only how Moltmann has modified the historicality of the Trinity as suggested in *The Crucified God*, but also how far he has now moved from the 'unlinear' emphasis on the *future* of God which Barth had criticised in the early Moltmann.

The history of God with the world is not, however, to be thought of as no more than a manifestation of what God is already in himself in eternity. God really opens himself for experience of history (*CPS* p. 56). Moltmann still wishes to maintain an important element of historical becoming in God in his history with men. For this reason, the trinitarian history of God is not sufficiently described by the inference to the 'Trinity in the origin'. It must also be understood from a future perspective towards its goal, for if the experience of history is real for God the eschatological Trinity will not be the same as the 'Trinity in the origin'. Moltmann holds that theological tradition has stressed too exclusively the backward perspective from the history of Christ through the Incarnation to this origin in the immanent Trinity. This perspective, though valid in itself, must be supplemented by the forward perspective through his resurrection to the eschatological goal of the Christ event (*CPS* p. 57).

This goal Moltmann calls the 'Trinity in the glorification'. 'Glory' is the biblical term for the divine splendour in which the whole creation is to participate in the End. In eschatological perspective the history of Christ and the history of the Spirit are movements of the glorification of God: the glorification of the Father by the Son and the glorification of the Father and the Son by the Spirit – which is at the same time the glorification of men, since God is glorified only in the liberation of his creation.

This glorification of God in the liberation of his creation takes place by the inclusion of creation within the divine life.

Jürgen Moltmann

Moltmann pictures God opening himself in seeking love in the mission of the Son and the Spirit, and then in gathering love in the work of the Spirit gathering the whole creation into union with himself.

It follows, claims Moltmann, that the *unity* of God must be differently conceived in the 'Trinity in the origin' and the 'Trinity in the glorification'. The unity of God in the 'Trinity in the origin' is 'that which is ontologically the foundation of the sendings of Son and Spirit': Moltmann declines to specify how this unity is to be understood (*CPS* p. 61). But the unity of God in his eschatological goal 'contains within itself the whole union of creation with God and in God' (*CPS* p. 61). This unity corresponds to the eschatological 'panentheism' of *The Crucified God* (277). 'If the unity of God were described in the doctrine of the Trinity by *koinonia* instead of by *una natura*, this idea would not seem so unusual' (*CPS* p. 62).

Finally Moltmann comments further on the historical experience of God. 'By opening himself for this history and entering into it . . . God also experiences the history of this world in its breadth and depth' (*CPS* p. 62). As Moltmann already claimed in *The Crucified God*, this history is for God not only an experience of the world but also an experience of himself, in that the events between the persons of the Trinity cannot leave the relationships between the persons absolutely the same as before.

God's experience of history 'has two sides to it'. From the sending of the Son to the cross, he *experiences* history as suffering, death and hell. From the resurrection to the End, he experiences joy in the *creation* of history.

God experiences history in order to create history. He goes out of himself in order to gather things to himself. He is vulnerable, he takes suffering and death upon himself in order to heal, to liberate, and to impart his eternal life. Out of this the resurrection gains a tendential predominance over the cross, exaltation over humiliation, and the joy of God over his pain. As a consequence the Trinity in the glorification has the predominance and the prominence before the Trinity in the sending. Formally it corresponds to the Trinity in the sending but in terms of content it reaches beyond the Trinity in the sending, just as the gathering love of God corresponds to the seeking love of God and yet through the gathering together and unification of humanity and the world with God reaches far beyond the seeking love of God. (*Theol* p. 645).

Thus God's experience of history results in an enrichment of the trinitarian being of God himself.

VI. THE TRINITARIAN BEING OF GOD

If Moltmann began by giving eschatology the role which Barth gave to the doctrine of the Trinity, he ends by reaching something of a synthesis of the two. God is no longer located exclusively in the future, but the future retains a kind of predominance. The future goal of the history of the world is the future goal of God himself, who through his history with the world becomes more than he was in his eternity without the world. The validity of Barth's inference to the immanent Trinity is admitted, but the economic Trinity is protected from being understood as an 'epiphany of the eternal present' by the claim that the historical process has creative significance for the trinitarian being of God himself.

Moltmann's doctrine of the Trinity remains a sketch. Its central problem – the meaning of temporality for God – remains obscure, and Moltmann has not explained his retreat from the extreme suggestions of *The Crucified God*[6] to the milder position of *The Church in the Power of the Spirit*.

Moltmann has scarcely discussed the classic problems of trinitarian doctrine. He speaks of three 'persons' without attempting to define the term. Indeed, his claim in *The Crucified God* that 'God' is the event between the three persons seems to assume that whereas the term 'God' is problematic and ambiguous, the term 'person' is not. Moltmann's second person is the human person of Jesus, but does the term mean the same when applied to the Father, whose identity is left wholly obscure in the claim that 'God' is the name for an event, and to the Spirit, of which Moltmann always speaks in impersonal terms?

The unity of God Moltmann defines as community of will (*FH* p. 27; *CG* p. 244), where this is said to be the meaning of the *homoousion*) or as *koinonia* (*CPS* p. 42), in the latter case potentially including creation in its unity. Are these statements sufficient to distinguish Moltmann's doctrine from tritheism? Moltmann is more concerned to distinguish his doctrine from philosophical theism and 'general religious monotheism' (*CG* p. 236) and even from Islamic monotheism (*CG* p. 250) – since these have objectionable anthropological implications – but he ought at least to be interested in its continuity with Jewish (Old Testament) monotheism, for Moltmann is entirely clear that the Father of Jesus Christ is the God of Israel (*TH* p. 141, *CG* p. 150) and his theology is notable for stressing the normativity of Old Testament theology for interpreting the New. If the cross is not to be understood by reference to a concept of God imported from elsewhere (*CG* p. 190), it must nevertheless presuppose the God of the Old Testament. Moltmann indeed claims that 'Christian faith does not have a new idea of God, but rather finds itself in a different God-situation' (*EH* p. 78), but his explanation of this is limited to finding some Old Testament precedent for a 'dual personality' of God in his suffering history with his people, according to Abraham

Richard Bauckham

Heschel's interpretation of the prophets (*CG* pp. 270–4). The sketch of the trinitarian history of God in *The Church in the Power of the Spirit* simply begins with the Incarnation. We miss Moltmann's rather thorough attention to Old Testament theology in other contexts (e.g. *TH* ch. 2). The new 'God-situation' of the cross, if it does not produce a 'new idea of God', requires much closer correlation with the old idea of the one God of Israel.

University of Manchester   RICHARD BAUCKHAM

NOTES

1. Page references are given with the following abbreviations for Moltmann's works in English translation:
   TH = *Theology of Hope* (London, 1967).
   RRF = *Religion, Revolution and the Future* (New York, 1969).
   FH = 'Theology as Eschatology', *The Future of Hope*, ed. F. Herzog (New York, 1970), pp. 1–50.
   Conc = 'The "Crucified God": God and the Trinity Today', *Concilium* no. 8, vol. 6 (1972), pp. 26–37.
   Int = 'The "Crucified God": A Trinitarian Theology of the Cross', *Interpretation* 26 (1972), pp. 278–99.
   CG = *The Crucified God* (London, 1974).
   EH = *The Experiment Hope* (London, 1975).
   Theol = 'The Trinitarian History of God', *Theology* 78 (1975), pp. 632–46.
   CPS = *The Church in the Power of the Spirit* (London, 1977).
2. I have had access only to the French translation of these letters between Barth and Moltmann, in *Études théologiques et religieuses* 101 (1976), pp. 167–170.
3. 'Theology as Eschatology', *The Future of Hope*, ed. F. Herzog, pp. 1–50; 'Hope and History', *RRF*, pp. 200–220.
4. Some of the relevant material in *CG* also appears in slightly different forms in three articles: 'The "Crucified God": God and the Trinity Today', *Concilium* no. 8 vol. 6 (1972), pp. 26–37; 'The "Crucified God": A Trinitarian Theology of the Cross', *Interpretation* 26 (1972), pp. 278–

299; 'The Crucified God', *Theology Today* 31 (1974–5), pp. 6–18 (= 'The Crucified God and Apathetic Man', *EH* pp. 69–84).

5. This reappears with a little additional material in 'The Trinitarian History of God', *Theology* 78 (1975), pp. 632–646.

6. Cf. here the criticism in G. Hunsinger, 'The Crucified God and the Political Theology of Violence', *Heythrop Journal* 14 (1973), pp. 278f.

CHAPTER NINE

Process Theology

Alfred North Whitehead (1861–1947) was not a theologian. He was a scholar who spent his lifetime labouring in the fields of mathematics and philosophy. His first important book, published with Bertrand Russell in 1913, was a treatise in logic and mathematics entitled *Principia Mathematica*. The *magnum opus* of his mature years was *Process and Reality* (1929), one of the few important metaphysical works of the twentieth century. It is perhaps somewhat surprising then, that his work has had such an impact on theology. The surprise, however, diminishes when one considers the monumental dimensions of his philosophical task. What Whitehead attempted to do was work out a new understanding of reality for the modern West. Whether or not he accomplished this is a side issue at this point; it is the attempt itself which is so impressive. And for those theologians who believe that he was indeed successful, his work provides a conceptual frame-work in which the historic christian faith can be re-thought and re-stated for our own time. Such thinkers make up the school known as Process Theology. Their work draws not only on the philosophical vision of Whitehead, but also on that of Charles Hartshorne, who, while clearly his own man, is one of the chief living exponents of Whitehead's Process Philosophy.

In this essay I shall attempt four things. First, I will explain those concepts of Whitehead's Process Philosophy which are relevant to the work of theology. Secondly, I will show how Process theologians apply these concepts to the development of theological doctrines, and follow this with a discussion of a specific christian doctrine, the Holy Trinity. Finally, I will offer a brief philosophical critique of this theological position.

It should be clear from the outset that Process Theology is without apology a *philosophical* theology. The claim here is that if theologians are to be honest, they must face the fact that they cannot avoid working within the context of a particular conceptual scheme or world view. Augustine openly embraced neo-Platonism and constructed his impressive theological edifice using its materials. Thomas Aquinas worked with the Aristotelianism of his time. The world views of other theologians have been less obvious or articulate, but they are none the less present. What all of this comes to is the view that the issue for theology is not so much whether or not to be guided by philosophy, but of finding the right philosophy.[1]

Another important initial point to make is that Process theologians reject the sharp distinction between general and special revelation that characterises most Protestant theology. Commitment to this distinction, they claim, results in an artificial polarisation of theology. While it may be true that there is a difference of *emphasis* between generalised philosophical theology and more specialised biblical theology, each is influenced by God's special revelation in history and his general revelation in nature and in human experience. This is not to say that Process Theology de-emphasises God's revelation in Jesus Christ. On the contrary an understanding of the historical event of Jesus Christ, and the first human response to him, i.e., the early Church, is viewed as central to the task of theology. The Church must always look back to him and to the early Church in its efforts to construct a systematic account of its beliefs. In the life of

James D. Spiceland

individuals and in the life of the Church, being christian means making the 'Jesus-event' central in all of life and in theology as well. But the Church must also recognise God's work in nature and in society. The Church must work out her 'self-understandings in the larger . . . categories of secular experience'.[2] The sharp distinction, then, between general and special revelation is a false one. Both are necessary and complementary to one another in carrying out the theological task of the Church.

I. SOME PHILOSOPHICAL CONCEPTS

As process theologian Bernard Lee has stated it, 'If one were allowed but a single statement in which to characterise Whitehead's philosophy, it would surely have to be that process itself is the reality'.[3] The world as we know it is in a constant state of evolution, of movement, of becoming. Now this does not mean that *everything* is changing, i.e., that even the principle of change itself is subject to change. The basic principles of process are unchanging. But having made that logical point we must go on to assert that reality is in process. Everything is in process and everything is interrrelated. Man is a part of nature and we, along with nature, are changing. And this changing is not the mere re-arranging of atoms like the reshuffling of cards. It is a process which engenders genuine novelty, an epigenetic movement. This notion of epigenetic movement is especially important. For Whitehead, referring to the world as 'creation' was not simply an example of religious jargon. It referred to a basic metaphysical presupposition. The world really is creation, a creative process which is full of novelty. Historical events bring change, and we as individuals are constantly growing and maturing. In nature we find that continents drift, new species evolve and weather patterns change, yet, as the Catholic poet, Gerard Manley Hopkins has said,

> And for all this, nature is never spent;
> There lives the dearest freshness deep down things.[4]

Whitehead's metaphysic asserts that the entire temporal process is a becoming, a transition from one event to another. These events are 'actual entities', and they begin to perish as soon as they come into being. An analogy with a motion picture may be helpful in grasping this. The picture gives the appearance of a continual flow, but in actuality it is a series of distinct frames.[5] These distinct frames or actual entities are all closely interrelated, yet they are individuals. In fact, they are the genuine individuals of reality. The sorts of things that we might call individuals, i.e., things that endure through time, are not the real individuals, but are 'societies' of these momentary experiences. Personal human existence, for instance, is a serially ordered society of occasions of experience.[6] In this metaphysical sense, I am not now the man I was ten years ago, nor will I be the same man ten years from now – I am changing, growing, becoming, sometimes as C. S. Lewis said, becoming 'surprised by joy'.

At the deepest level, even these actual entities which constitute the temporal process are themselves processes, the processes of their own individual becoming. From the external perspective they may appear to happen all at once, but actually they do not endure through a minute bit of time; rather they take that bit of time to become. The Whiteheadean term for this minute becoming is 'concrescence', i.e., becoming concrete. And here the motion picture analogy mentioned above loses its usefulness, as the individual pictures are static entities whereas Whitehead's individual occasions are dynamic acts of concrescence. We can see from this that at the most basic levels, reality is in process. It is dynamic and not static. The smallest actual occasion is itself a process of becoming.

Closely tied to the concept of process is the concept of relatedness. I have already noted that the things which we see as enduring in time are actually a series of occasions of experience. Examples of such entities from physics would be electrons and molecules. And in the human realm, what theologians call the soul is also characterised by a series of distinct occasions of experience.

Enduring individuals, however, are not independent and separable. Each moment of experience is related to what went before in an essential way. These individuals are not primarily individual things which happen to enter into relations with others. On the contrary, the relations are primary. In Whitehead's technical language the terms for these relations are 'prehension' and 'feeling'. Each present occasion 'prehends', it grasps, the previous occasions. In fact, the present occasion really consists in its process of unifying the prehensions with which it begins. It has its geneses in past occasions and it becomes the 'stuff' of future occasions. The practical outcome of this is the view that all 'individuals' are interrelated. In the theological context a natural application of this philosophical notion is a strong emphasis on interdependence as opposed to independence, and hence on community. The Church is an interdependent community in which each part is closely related to other parts and all must work together to achieve its purpose. It is a body, not a machine, and the functioning of the body is dependent on the functioning of each part. Now it is true that the biblical view of man has had some influence in the development of the modern West's emphasis on the importance of the individual. But it is equally true that the modern view has gone far beyond the biblical view, which understands man as essentially belonging to a community, as growing, developing, creating his identity in *relation* to other human beings, the world, and God. Process Theology adopts the relational emphasis of Process Philosophy and maintains that this is in support of the biblical understanding of man, God, and the world.

A third philosophical notion that is germane to theology is the notion of incarnation. This serves to underscore Whitehead's emphasis on interrelatedness. Occasions of experience are related to each incarnationally, i.e., past experiences are incorporated into present experiences. Present experiences include past experiences. Two logical observations are in order here.[7] First, the inclusion of the past experience must be selective and limited, for to include the whole experience as present is to confuse past and present. Secondly, the present experience cannot include the past as still experiencing. The past, as such, is present only as *having been* an experience.

The most obvious example of this is memory. When we remember a past experience, the memory is partly constitutive of our present experience. Clearly the totality of the past experience is not included in the memory, only some of its content, and some of its subjective reaction to that content. So the past experience is in the present experience objectively. The past lives on in the present objectively, and in this way is incarnated in the present. For Whitehead this was the 'objective immortality of the past'.

A final philosophical concept to be clarified is the Process view of experience. It was Sigmund Freud who likened consciousness to the tip of an iceberg, and Process thought is in agreement with this understanding. Whitehead's claim was that 'consciousness presupposes experience and not experience consciousness'.[8] A great deal of our experience is at the prereflective, or pre-thematised level. It is at this level of preconscious experience that many of the ultimate issues of our lives have their genesis. And this level of experience has a great influence on the direction and quality of our conscious experience. We have, for instance, a primordial awareness of ultimate reality, and this contact with reality is the source of all genuine creativity in our lives. It is here that the quality and direction of our lives are shaped. For reasons which Process thinkers do not always make clear, only a few individuals in a particular culture or historical era are able to harness fully the energies released in these basic experiences. They become the great intellectual and cultural leaders, the poets, mathematicians, and mystics of history. Their contributions at the conscious level enrich and deepen the experiences of all of us. But we are able to give assent and become enriched by their work only because it strikes a chord of harmony at the deepest levels of all of us. The great literary classics of our civilisation are great because in reading them we recognise truth – truth about nature, about mankind, and truth about ourselves. This recognition is the result of a process of giving conscious expression to truths we are all aware of at the preconscious level of experience. The application of this Whiteheadean theme to theology should be fairly clear. A great deal of our important religious experiences take place at the level of pre-thematised experience. The great moral and religious 'systems' of mankind really have their origins here. This, of course, is extremely relevant to the development of religious doctrine, to which I shall now turn.

II. RELIGIOUS EXPERIENCE AND DOCTRINAL FORMULATIONS

True religion has its beginnings at the most profound levels of human experience. It has to do with our deepest longings for harmony with what is finally real. St Augustine's feeling that his heart was restless until it found the rest in fellowship with God is a clear expression of this theme. He found that there is a 'God-shaped void' in all of us. The emphasis of Process Theology is very similar to this. Their claim is that we all have a preconscious knowledge of God – in fact, we all *know* that there is this sacred reality and that in the end it makes all the difference as far as the meaning of our lives is concerned. It is, of course, possible by the use of artificial logical techniques, for us to be argued out of our belief in God, but this only demonstrates that at times our conscious beliefs can be in tension with what we know to be true at the pre-reflective level. Hence the biblical observation, 'The fool has said in his heart there is no God'. His foolishness consists not in some moral perversity but in his persistence in a conscious belief which conflicts with his basic experience of reality. Such a belief prevents an integrated life, because the basic structure of reality will always impose itself on us in spite of conscious beliefs that might be in conflict with it. A particularly illustrative example of the possibility of conflict between conscious belief and pre-reflective experience centres on the notion of causality.[9] It is a matter of universal pre-reflective knowledge that the present is causally influenced by the past rather than being merely preceded by it. But certain thinkers have been 'argued out' of this view of causality. Their claim is that what is generally called 'efficient causation' is actually only 'constant conjunction'. Believers in efficient causation, they say, have been bewitched into believing in some magical causal relationship between events on the mere evidence of temporal sequence. Process Philosophy holds, however, that such a conscious belief does not ring true with experience, no matter how firmly it is held. Those who verbally deny efficient causation reveal in their everyday lives that they know differently.

They have beliefs, say, about responsibility, and they act on these beliefs. They save money, by insurance policies, and pay their debts. This presupposes that some events influence others, i.e., that latter events *would not* have happened without the former. The emotional side of life also implies efficient causation. Emotions such as guilt and anger presuppose real influence between various actions, attitudes, and beliefs. To put it in a more pragmatic vein, such a belief simply does not work. It does not work because it is in conflict with what is experienced as true at the preconscious level. We cannot escape the basic structure of reality. And of course, this carries over into man's religious experiences. Judaeo-christian literature has many accounts of men who struggle with God. The biblical point is always that we must align our beliefs and practices with our experience of God. The sacred reality will always extract an appropriate response from us in spite of conscious beliefs which may conflict with it.

Now all of this is very relevant to the development of religious doctrine, as doctrine is a form given to our consciously held beliefs. It is extremely important that our doctrinal statements accurately express our pre-reflective experience. Whitehead pointed out that ideas have a life of their own, i.e., they have a dynamic influence on our inner lives. Once they are accepted and vividly held before the mind they have a way of becoming entrenched in our psyches. Foundational beliefs concerning the meaning and purpose of existence, our relation to the sacred reality, etc., which are held deeply and over a long period of time have a great deal of force in the shaping of moral and spiritual character. One's general emotional and behavioural outlook is deeply influenced by the doctrines one believes in on these ultimate issues. This means that Process Theology, unlike some contemporary theological stances, takes doctrinal issues seriously. Doctrine is important although the reasons for its importance are somewhat different from those which might be given in a more traditional context. The importance of doctrine is related to psychic wholeness. I have already mentioned that according to Process thought, consciousness is based in experience and not vice versa. Every moment of conscious experience is influenced by preconscious experience. But reality is in constant process, and each actual occasion of experience is intimately related to what went before it and what follows it. So the influence of preconscious and conscious experience on one another is not all in one direction. The conscious affirmations of one moment may influence the quality of preconscious experience of the next. Pre-thematic experiences *are* influenced by the emergence of conscious beliefs. Consciousness and experience are dynamic interrelated processes. Any particular moment of human experience is substantively influenced by previous moments of experience, including the *conscious* elements of those experiences. This interrelatedness means that over a long period of time, one's total relation to reality can be influenced by one's conscious beliefs. What this all comes to with reference to religious doctrine is the point that conscious beliefs must harmonise with our deep experience of God. If our conscious beliefs are in conflict with the universal pre-conscious experience of reality, we are broken within ourselves. There is tension between what we consciously affirm on the one hand and our preconscious experience on the other. This brokenness, this lack of psychic wholeness, is not to be taken lightly, for it is a basic and profound brokenness of the human spirit. It is a brokenness which paralyses the human person in the spiritual sense. If we are to know spiritual wholeness, our conscious beliefs must 'fit in' with our primordial experience. This is one of the basic reasons why Process Theology takes doctrinal issues so seriously.

Another reason is related to the fact that religious experience and beliefs have to do with our relation to ultimate reality. They are rooted in our deepest longings and needs. They, therefore, have great potential for enriching our lives. Conscious beliefs which are in harmony with ultimate reality can work to effect spiritual wholeness, although this process may be extremely slow at times.

Concerning the affirmative effectiveness of correct doctrinal beliefs Whitehead has a most interesting discussion in his *Adventures of Ideas*. It is a discussion of the rise in ancient Greece, of the belief that all men have souls, are 'ensouled'. This belief rose to the level of conscious awareness in the midst of a culture which was wholly committed to the institution of slavery. Now to us the tension between this doctrine of ensoulment and slavery is obvious, but it was not so evident at first. Aristotle seems to have been only dimly aware of the inconsistencies, if at all. The doctrine of ensoulment, however, being in harmony with the race's basic apprehension of reality, survived and was strengthened by the rise and spread of Christianity. Over the centuries the preaching of the christian gospel with its attendant high view of all men as ensouled by God brought the inappropriateness of slavery into bold relief. The tension between the doctrine of ensoulment and the institution of slavery became increasingly influential in bringing about social, intellectual and spiritual unrest. This finally resulted in the 'settled policy of the great civilised governments to extirpate slavery from the world'.[10] The doctrine of ensoulment, which emerged into conscious expression so long ago, has been influential in bringing civilisation more into harmony with man's primordial awareness of reality. It has brought wholeness to the existence of individuals and to the life of a civilisation.

Another reason for the importance of doctrine in Process Theology relates to the fact that religious beliefs, in pertaining to ultimate moral and spiritual issues, influence our values and the general direction of our lives. They do this by selecting certain aspects of experience for emphasis and development. In the history of the christian Church we find a variety of doctrinal beliefs and emphasis. These doctrinal emphases have tended to select various aspects of christian experience which in turn have influenced the attitudes, purposes and general direction of the different christian traditions. Throughout christian history, there has been considerable diversity not only of doctrine, but of doctrinal emphasis. This has resulted in a diversity of theological traditions in the Church. Within this broad context differing doctrinal beliefs and emphasis has resulted in a variety of christian experiences. They may both be christian, but the character of christian experience in say, the Latin American Pentecostal context is different from the experience found and encouraged among German Lutherans. With reference to the doctrine of the Trinity, a plausible argument can be developed which claims that an emphasis on God the Father and his attributes, at the expense of the other two persons in the Trinity, has tended to result in a stern and 'other worldly' Christianity. These christian traditions sometimes over-emphasise a legalistic morality and select God's authority, justice and wrath for emphasis. This clearly produces a particular type of christian experience which can be observed in various christian traditions. An emphasis on God the Son at the expense of the other two persons of the Godhead, sometimes results in a kind of 'humanism in Christian dress'. With respect to trinitarian doctrine, Norman Pittenger, himself a Process theologian, has lamented the de-emphasis of the third person in trinitarian belief and practice. The Holy Spirit, he says, has been treated as a 'poor relation',[11] and this has resulted in, among other things, the Church beginning to resemble a machine, rather than a body, the correct biblical image. And so we observe

the rise of the great ecclesiastical machine with its attendant
bureaucracy. It is, in some cases, very orthodox and proper,
but it is nevertheless a dead orthodoxy and does not generate
a spiritual response from living men. This is at least partly
because the Church has ignored or de-emphasised the work
of the Holy Spirit of God in its midst. It has failed to allow the
doctrine to do its work.

Another example of what I would call the selective force of
doctrinal beliefs has to do with morality. According to
Process Philosophy, moral concepts are rooted in a universal
impulse to moral activity. But the moral impulse has clearly
enjoyed more development in some philosophical traditions
than in others. Moral ideas which are in harmony with our
pre-reflective experience and rise to the level of conscious
awareness tend to produce psychic wholeness. It stands to
reason that a belief which holds that morality is embedded in
the very nature of things will treat moral issues with great
seriousness. The world-view which perceives morality as
central, therefore, gives a different quality to experience than
one which sees morality as peripheral.

Human experience, as we have seen, is infinitely complex.
Out of this complexity, philosophical and moral teachings
select certain elements to be lifted into the arena of conscious
affirmation and thereby into increased effectiveness in our
lives. Those christian doctrines which relate to our universal
awareness of the sacred reality are efficacious in the same
way. They elevate certain aspects of that universal awareness
to the level of consciousness, and this conscious affirmation
influences our purposes and commitments, engendering a
greater degree of spiritual wholeness.[12]

In speaking of the emergence of doctrinal beliefs into the
level of conscious awareness, I should point out that doctrine
always develops in historical and linguistic communities.
Christian doctrine, as a linguistic description of pre-

thematised universal experience, always involves some interpretation. Language is never entirely neutral. All language, no matter how great the attempt at objectivity, is shaped by its own history, by the philosophical presuppositions, conceptual schemes, etc., of those who speak it. And the fact that human beings enjoy a certain amount of freedom with respect to their response to experience means that different people may respond to identical features of reality in different ways. What this comes to is the view that, although man's primordial experience of God may be the same, people of different ages, cultures, and language groups will express their response to this experience differently. So different stories get told, depending on culture, time, etc., and different modes of expression are employed to tell those stories. The linguistic expression of religious belief is therefore very diverse. And different linguistic expressions of religious experience give rise to different religious traditions, each bearing, to some extent, the marks of the cultural, historical, and linguistic communities in which it grew. In discussing religious experience and language, Whitehead spoke of a 'community of intuition'. A community of intuition consists of two groups. First, it contains those few great religious geniuses who express 'completely novel intuitions'.[13] These are the prophets, the mystics, the founders, of the great historical religions. Their words are recorded as the foundation of all doctrinal expressions of those religions. Secondly, communities of intuition include those who respond to the founders. These are the disciples and apostles of the great religious geniuses whose writings record the experiences of the founders. History has only a few great mystics, men who have genuinely novel intuitions of reality. But their lives evoke a response, a response which cannot go beyond 'those definite intuitions which they flashed upon the world'[14] but which is an interpretation, an effort to put the

experiences and ideas of the great mystics into language and
thus pass them on. For Process Theology, these mystics and
those who become their apostles are extremely important in
the development of doctrine. Their lives and times are the
context in which doctrines have their genesis. And their
language, thought-forms, and world-views get passed on in
recording the mystics' experiences of God. These languages
therefore continue to have influence in the formation of
doctrine since they carry their world-view along from
generation to generation. This then, is another way in which
doctrinal beliefs influence religious experience. They
continually instill and re-instill a certain perspective and
thereby influence the tenor of our religious experience. We
see this in the fact that some religious traditions are considered to be more 'Greek' in their philosophical perspective,
others are more 'Hebraic'. Religious truth is found in all
these traditions but the character of religious experience
varies from one tradition to another.

A note of caution about doctrine is relevant here. It must
always be remembered that the great religions of the world
have their genesis in experience. This experience is the
'content' of religion, doctrinal statements the 'form' in which
it is passed on. Preoccupation with doctrinal statements will
inevitably result in an emulation of the thought forms, world-
views, etc., of other times and places. 'You cannot claim
absolute finality for a dogma without claiming a com-
mensurate finality for the sphere of thought in which it
arose.'[15] This will produce a dead orthodoxy in which an
insistence on correct doctrinal statements will actually become a stumbling block to those who are seeking genuine
religious experience in their own time. The French Process
philosopher Henri Bergson said, 'a doctrine which is but a
doctrine has a poor chance indeed of giving birth to the
glowing enthusiasm, the illumination, the faith that moves

mountains'.[16] Doctrine, then, is of great importance, but its importance is derived from the fact that it is a description of a pre-thematised experience of God. It should be seen as an outward sign of 'an inward and spiritual grace'.[17] It must never be allowed to become, in and of itself, the primary focus of religious or even theological attention. If it does, the result is idolatry.[18]

In this section I have attempted to clarify the Process theologian's understanding of what religious doctrine is, how it develops, and the role it plays in the ongoing life of religion. In what follows I shall attempt to relate all of this to a particular christian doctrine, the doctrine of the Holy Trinity.

III. THE TRINITY IN PROCESS THOUGHT

Theologians, like the rest of us, are sometimes given to fads. And of late it has become something of a fad, at least among English-speaking thinkers, to doubt the usefulness or accuracy of certain ancient doctrines, including the doctrine of the Trinity. 'What sense can modern man make of it?' is a common question nowadays. And some, with a tinge of condescension, claim that all we can honestly do with it is retain the old language, viewing it as a picturesque and useful symbol which links us with the past, while at the same time recognising that trinitarian talk can no longer be taken seriously. It is an interesting and possibly poetically valuable relic, but not quite relevant to our world, and theology must be, by all means, relevant. It is appropriate, I think, to say at the outset of this discussion that Process theologians do not take this view. The Trinity, like other doctrinal formulations of the christian faith, must be taken seriously. It is a doctrine which provides us with genuine insight into the divine reality. It is true that these Christians generally feel that some of the spirited debates of the past, which usually centred on logical precision and other linguistic details, were ill conceived. But the doctrinal formulation which emerged from early debates and councils is a genuine expression of the divine self-revelation to man. Those who treat it lightly do so at the cost of impoverishing their own understanding of the Faith.

The view that the real point of this doctrine is its logical meaning is a wrong-headed one. Indeed, trinitarian thinking is not the kind of theorising which delights logical and philosophical minds. It is rather an effort to give conscious expression and make sense of a living reality, 'which is the inescapable fact, the absolute heart and centre, of Christianity'.[19] The point of the doctrine, then, as with all doctrines, is to express and emphasise certain aspects of the divine reality. It is intended to give significance to christian life and worship. This is brought into sharp focus in the Athanasian Creed's statement, 'This is the Catholic faith: that we *worship* one God in Trinity and Trinity in unity'. It is not merely a speculative effort. It is the result of a serious attempt on the part of early Christians to grapple with what the knowledge of God in Jesus Christ and the fellowship of the Holy Spirit must imply about the nature of God. The Scriptures tell us that God was in Christ reconciling the world to himself. Early Christians not only grasped this concept with their minds, they *experienced* it. And their experience was that to know God in Christ was to be 'in the Spirit'. To experience the love of God in Christ was to experience the Spirit at work in the life of the believer. Clearly this is not material for the static categories of logic. It is the experience of a dynamic reality, and the trinitarian formulations were an attempt to express and preserve the threefold experience of God in Christ through the Spirit. The entire apparatus of technical language about the Trinity results from the attempt '. . . of the Christian fathers to make sense of *Christian life*'.[20]

In the earlier discussion of the basic concepts of Process Philosophy it was pointed out that the world and all that is in it are in the process of becoming. This becoming is a movement toward realisation of potentiality. Each individual occasion of experience has a purpose. And all occasions of experience are interrelated. For the Christian, who sees all of this process as the creation of God, the dominant factor is the purpose of God. He gives meaning, direction and energy to each occasion of experience and to us as enduring individuals. He is a God of love and is intimately related to every part of creation, as it comes into existence and moves toward fulfilment. He is the vital impetus which energises all process, and at the same time he lures all of creation toward himself. God draws all of creation, even inorganic matter, ('even the rocks cry out') toward himself by his love. He shares in the sorrows of creation as well as its joys, he incarnates himself in the entire process as he faithfully works to help everything realise its proper good.

At the human level he wishes to have a personal relationship with each individual, and those of us who are Christians claim that Jesus Christ is the unique example, in the entire process of history, of divine self-disclosure. In personal responses to God's love expressed in him, Christians discover that they have inner strength to move toward realisation of their fullest human potential. Each Christian is an individual yet he or she is intimately related to all other members of the body of Christ. And all experience this inner strength in response to Christ. For us who are human beings then, the force which moves us toward the fulfilment of all our potential is a strength found in response to Christ.

It is in the context of this experience that trinitarian formula begins to make sense. The complete truth about the nature of an infinite God cannot be grasped by the finite mind of man. But we can catch a glimpse of God's nature as he reveals himself to us. Trinitarian doctrine is an effort to express clearly that 'glimpse' in language. If Process theologians have any criticisms of the Church Fathers who worked out the trinitian expression, it is not that they were inaccurate, but that they claimed far more precise knowledge than any finite mind can ever have about the mystery of the divine nature. In spite of this, their formulation has stood the test of hundreds of years of corporate and individual christian experience. For the individual Christian and for the Church, this doctrine has been definitive in gaining an understanding of who God is, what he is like, and how, with our limited intellects, we can best conceive of him and his action.

The christian experience of God has always been three-fold. First of all, God is active in the world in that he is that agency which gives to each entity its initial aim. Each entity has its own unique aim, and this means that there is genuine novelty in creation. Each individual in the body of Christ is indeed an individual, with a certain potential to realise, a potential that is given by God. We are his workmanship, created in order that we may realise everything which he intended for each of us. This is the christian experience of God as the ultimate source or cause.[21]

Secondly, this experience is that an entity has not only an initial aim to fulfil, it also has a pattern of fulfilment or a path it must follow if it is to satisfy its initial aim. At all levels of existence, God ordains the pattern which is in keeping with his will. This pattern is the direction that each entity must take if it is to reach full realisation of its potential. Christians believe, and their experience confirms, that in human life, the God-given path is found in the life of Jesus Christ. His life, which was lived in a particular historical context and which brought about certain effects in the world, is for Christians, the '. . . visible human expression of the divine intention. It is the self-expression of the divine purpose for the human race.'[22] The event of Jesus Christ is this and it is more. Christians believe that in Christ they see the self-expression, not only of the divine purpose, but of the divine himself. The man Jesus Christ as Son of God and son of man is the self-expression of the divine that man can understand. The divine reality is self-expressive at every level of creation, and it is self-expressive in ways which make it available for reception by each particular level. Christians believe that at the human level the self-expression of God which is available is seen in the life of Jesus Christ, God the Son.

The third aspect of the christian experience of God has to do with man's response to God's action and expression. Each entity in creation receives its initial aim from God, and also has some knowledge of the way in which that aim can be fulfilled. That way of fulfilment is both an expression of the individual's identity and an expression of the divine purpose for it. Each entity is enabled to give its assent to the fulfilment of its essential aim. This 'enablement' is the result of God's working within the entity and also of his total work in the world. The experience of Christians is that they are energised by God in their response to his love. In a manner which they may not be able to articulate with great clarity, they sense that even in their response to God, he is at work within them. And quite clearly in the christian life their experience is that God is at work within them, working his own will. This is God the Spirit, working to bring about the full realisation of the Christian's potential which is the will of God.

In this discussion of christian experience, the three modes of God's activity, and the interrelationship of the same, are brought into sharp focus. God is the creative source or cause in that he provides the initial aim. He is God the creator. He

draws men to the realisation of their potential by providing
the pattern of self-expression, and finally he urges men toward himself and in this he works for the response which will
enable his creatures to become all that they are capable of
being. So Christians experience God as Creative Source, as
Self-Expressive Act, and Responsive Movement. And they
experience him as one God. This is 'trinitarianism',[23] the
basis of the doctrine of the Trinity.

The entire emphasis of the Process view of doctrine is on
experience. Doctrine is an attempt to formulate our preconscious experiences of God. This means that all doctrinal
beliefs must be personal beliefs. To worship God as the
Trinity means, in the final analysis, that each of us as
Christians experiences God as the source of all that is fresh
and meaningful in our lives. He gives to us our purpose. Our
experience of God also tells each of us that our ultimate
purpose can only be realised when the pattern for our living
becomes the man who was God's self-expression in history,
Jesus Christ. He alone is the full realisation of a human being
while truly divine. And finally to worship God the Trinity is
to be open to the refreshing wind of his Spirit within us, to
know his power in quickening us, in bringing about a
response of love to all that he is. To worship God as the
Trinity is to have a personal christian knowledge of God.

IV. PHILOSOPHICAL CRITIQUE

At a practical and somewhat uncritical level, Process
Theology has some wholesome contributions to make to the
life of the Church. Its emphasis on the christian life as a
constant process of growth and development is, while not
altogether new, certainly an important one. The strong
emphasis on the relation of doctrine and experience is
extremely valuable, especially in those quarters of the

Church which have over-emphasised correct doctrine and thereby tended to produce a lifeless Christianity, a 'dead orthodoxy'. With special reference to the doctrine of the Trinity, Pittenger's call for a rediscovery of the person and work of the Holy Spirit in the ongoing life of the Church is refreshing and biblical. And of course the view that the Trinity is the absolute heart and centre of Christianity is in keeping with the historic orthodox understanding of what christian theology is all about. At this level then, Process Theology has much to offer.

At a more theoretical and basic level, however, I believe that this theological perspective has one flaw which seriously undermines its logical credibility. This flaw has its genesis in Whitehead's philosophical view that consciousness pre-supposes experience and not experience consciousness. The theological application of this view is the notion that christian doctrine is a conscious, articulate expression of a preconcious or 'pre-thematic' experience of God. The claim is that at the preconscious level we all *know* that there is this sacred reality, and doctrines result from the effort to articulate and formalise this preconscious knowledge. Religious doctrine is important because it is a conscious expression of this preconscious knowledge and from this we can infer that doctrines are judged to be true or false (or at least adequate or inadequate) in terms of whether or not they are in harmony with out preconscious knowledge. It is precisely here that the rub comes, for it appears to me that as long as the criteria for judging the truth or falsity of doctrine lies below the level of articulate expression, we can never make the judgment that a particular doctrine *contradicts* our preconscious experience and therefore is a false doctrine. What would count as a contradiction? Surely not some verbal expression of disagreement. As soon as we verbalise our *reason*, we are involved in conscious, thematic, rational

James D. Spiceland

discourse. What was alleged to be preconscious has emerged into the level of the conscious. The judgment that one idea contradicts another requires the comparison of two consciously formulated propositions, i.e., it is rational activity, and rationalising, by definition, is conscious activity. My point is that as long as the criteria for judging truth or falsity in religious debates is asserted to lie below the level of consciousness, all rational and verbal discussion of the adequacy of a doctrine is self-destructive. One might have a preconscious 'feeling' that doctrine is false, but to 'articulate' this feeling is to make it conscious – again, by definition.

Now I am aware of the fact that Process theologians do talk about 'feelings' and the emotive side of christian experience. And they also caution us that the doctrine of the Trinity, for instance, is not material for precise logical and philosophical analysis.

This judgment itself is part of their verbal response to the 'nit-picking' of some of the early Church Fathers. In the end, however, neither they nor these early Fathers can avoid some logical analysis, 'nit-picking' or not. Not at least if we are to talk about and make judgments concerning the truth or falsity of our doctrinal beliefs. This is not to say that 'nit-picking' is impossible or that philosophers (and theologians) never become unduly concerned with trivia. Clearly they do at times. But in insisting that the criteria of truth or falsity lies below the level of conscious expression, the Process theologians do much more than caution against a concern with logical trivia. They make judgments concerning the truth or falsity of doctrines impossible. This quite clearly is a ground very few theologians would wish to occupy. It is a kind of intellectual 'no-man's land'.

It is possible that within the logical boundaries of another theological perspective, one that did not make this difficult

155

appeal to preconscious experience, the emphasis and observations of Process Theology might be helpful. But within the
logical boundaries that Process theologians have attempted
to set for themselves, this perspective is, in my opinion, a
seriously flawed one. In the end, Process Philosophy turns
out to be an inadequate conceptual framework for the work of
theology.

Western Kentucky University   JAMES SPICELAND

NOTES

1. J. B. Cobb and D. R. Griffen, *Process Theology: An Introductory Exposition*
    (Philadelphia, 1976), p. 159.
2. Bernard Lee, *The Becoming of the Church* (New York, 1974), p. 172.
3. Lee, op. cit., p. 172.
4. X. J. Kennedy, *An Introduction to Poetry* (Boston, 1971), p. 153.
5. Cobb and Griffen, op. cit., p. 14.
6. Ibid., p. 15.
7. Ibid., p. 22.
8. Ibid., p. 17.
9. Ibid., p. 31.
10. Ibid., p. 33.
11. Norman Pittenger, *The Holy Spirit* (Philadelphia, 1974), p. 7.
12. Cobb and Griffen, op. cit., p. 36.
13. Alfred North Whitehead, *Religion in the Making* (New York, 1926), p.
    130.
14. Whitehead, op. cit., p. 130.
15. Ibid., p. 126.
16. Henri Bergson, *The Two Sources of Morality and Religion* (Westport,
    Connecticut, 1963), p. 226.
17. Whitehead, *Religion in the Making*, p. 127.
18. Ibid., p. 142.
19. Norman Pittenger, *The Holy Spirit*, p. 44.
20. Pittenger, op. cit., p. 44.
21. Ibid., p. 128.

22. Ibid., p. 123.
23. Ibid., p. 124

I wish to express my appreciation to my colleagues in the Department of Philosophy and Religion at Western Kentucky University for their valuable suggestions and criticism concerning the content of this essay.

CHAPTER TEN

Recent British Theology

The most striking feature of recent British trinitarian theology – at least where England is concerned – is the frankness with which orthodox trinitarianism is being questioned or even rejected. This sceptical note in doctrinal criticism has also been sounded over the doctrine of the Incarnation – not surprisingly; for the two doctrines are, both historically and rationally, linked. Indeed the collapse of trinitarian theology is an inevitable consequence of the abandonment of incarnational christology. Thus we find, in the writings of the Regius Professors of Divinity at the Universities of Oxford and Cambridge, Professors Maurice Wiles and Geoffrey Lampe, along with christological reductionism, a marked tendency towards unitarianism. Neither Wiles nor Lampe can see much future for the doctrine of the Trinity.[1]

It is perfectly true that both scholars are prepared to go on using trinitarian language, and they would certainly unite in rejecting deistic versions of unitarianism whereby God is thought of as remote and isolated from the world. Both would stress the immanence of God in his creation. But neither is prepared to grant much meaning, let alone an essential place in christian theism, to such classical formulations as that God is to be known and worshipped as three persons in one substance, or even to the looser affirmation that there exist relations of love within God.

Both Wiles and Lampe are liberal theologians. They have

affinities with turn of the century German 'Liberal Protestantism', as exemplified in the writings of Harnack and Troeltsch; but they are more characteristically English scholars and have more in common with the 'Modern Churchmen', whose Girton Conference of 1921 caused such a stir in British religious circles more than a generation ago. They share the clarity, the common sense and the rationalism of Bethune-Baker and Hastings Rashdall.

It is notable that Wiles and Lampe are both primarily patristic scholars. They are at home in the arguments of the early Christian Fathers, and yet have come to reject them on matters which they, the Fathers, thought to be central to, and of the essence of, the christian faith. It is also true to say that both scholars sit pretty lightly to the traditions of dogma, whether Catholic, Lutheran or Reformed, that come between the patristic age and our own.

There are differences between the two theologians. For one thing, Wiles' doctrinal criticism has been developed and sustained over a longer period of time and, one senses, in reaction against a once-held conservative theology of the Word. He restricts himself to hard-headed theological argument, relentlessly pressing the questions of meaning and truth. Lampe has moved more rapidly in recent years to an affirmation of minimal dogma, but from a long-held liberal Catholic position that is still sustained by sacramental piety. There is, in the Bampton Lectures, for all their critical stance towards the doctrines of the Incarnation and the Trinity, a wealth of mature spiritual insight.

Clarity is a great virtue, and the writings of Professors Wiles and Lampe are a pleasure to read. It is easy to understand what they are saying. There is no resort to rhetoric or bluster. The contrast between this calm reflective English theology and the dense and convoluted prose of many continental writers is very great. Yet the German theologians, with the major exception of the Bultmann school, and notwithstanding their awareness of the need to take the measure of Bultmann, remain obstinately, even excitingly, trinitarian. As will have appeared from other essays in the symposium, this is true of both Protestant and Catholic theology in Germany today. It is one of the ironies of the present theological scene that Liberal Protestantism has found a new lease of life in England at a time when it seems to have run its course in Germany.

This contrast between the clear and reasonable unitarianism of recent English theology and the dense and opaque trinitarianism of German theology has not always obtained. An earlier Oxford professor, Leonard Hodgson, writing with just such clarity, common sense and rationalism as are displayed by Wiles and Lampe, found himself driven to accept and to commend an orthodox trinitarian theology. 'The doctrine of the Trinity', he wrote, 'is the product of rational reflection on those particular manifestations of the divine activity which centre in the birth, ministry, crucifixion, resurrection and ascension of Jesus Christ, and the gift of the Holy Spirit to the Church . . . it could not have been discovered without the occurrence of those events, which drove human reason to see that they require a trinitarian God for their cause.'[2]

In discussing the work of Wiles and Lampe, we need to ask two main questions: in the first place, what are the reasons for their rejection of the trinitarian tradition? Secondly, how adequate are their non-trinitarian concepts of God? Or, put the other way round, what is lost from christian theism, when we cease to think in trinitarian terms?

The fact that these are the questions I wish to put to Wiles and Lampe shows that, to some extent, at least, I share their approach to theological problems. The doctrine of the Trinity cannot be established simply by citing authoritative

texts, whether of Scripture or tradition. Its primary source is
certainly divine revelation, but, as Leonard Hodgson saw,
revelation is a matter of events, of divine actions in human
history and in human lives. Revelation is not opposed to
reason. Part of our response to God's self-revealing acts is
precisely our rational reflection on the sense they make.

Already we are concerned with theological method, and
consideration of my first question – what are the reasons for
Wiles' and Lampe's dissatisfaction with the doctrine of the
Trinity? – must begin with the problem of method. So far I
have expressed agreement. We cannot take this doctrine
simply on authority. But when we look more closely at the
work of Wiles and Lampe, doubts on the score of method
begin to arise. It is Wiles who addresses himself most
explicitly to problems of theological method, but similar
procedures can be detected as being implicit in the work of
Lampe as well. In *The Remaking of Christian Doctrine,* Wiles
tells us that the two words that best describe his objective are
'coherence' and 'economy'.[3] I have no quarrel with the
criterion of coherence, though I shall argue shortly that
Lampe, at least, too readily supposes trinitarian theology to
be incoherent. My chief worry concerns 'economy'. The use
of this criterion is pervasive in both Wiles and Lampe. We
are not to postulate more doctrine than the evidence *demands.*
It was not *necessary* for the Fathers to erect the doctrinal
superstructure that they did in the way they did. Here are
two examples from Lampe: 'In order to interpret God's
saving work in Jesus we do not need the model of a descent of
a pre-existent divine person into the world'. 'If . . . it is God's
Spirit, his own real presence, which is active in and through
the reciprocal love and trust of human beings, then there is
no need to project human personality on to Trinitarian
"persons".'[4] I shall discuss the substance of this last quota-
tion later on. Here it simply illustrates the common use of the

criterion of 'economy'. We are to cut out all unnecessary theological accretions. This is a very dangerous criterion, especially when used alone. It is not surprising that, on this ground, unitarianism is preferred.

My objection is not to the criterion of economy as such, however. We should indeed consider what the evidence demands. Leonard Hodgson, in the passage quoted above, argued that the revelatory events *drove* human reason to see that they required a trinitarian God for their cause. My objection rather is to emphasise economy to the neglect of comprehensiveness. Before we appeal to what the evidence demands, we must be sure that we are taking account of *all* the evidence, that all the data are being scrutinised in all their relevant aspects. It is an objection to Wiles' method that he tends to take a particular patristic argument in isolation, show that it was not *necessary* to think that way, and conclude that christian theology would be better off without that particular doctrine. But by such a procedure one can easily miss much relevant evidence, and overlook the real reasons behind the Fathers' thinking. Considerations of economy and considerations of comprehensiveness must be weighed together. Nor is it just a question of historical evidence. It is a further objection to Wiles' use of his criterion of economy – though this does not apply to Lampe – that Wiles tends to think historically rather than theologically about the development of doctrine. We are to accept only what seems necessary to account for the historical evidence. But this is to neglect theological considerations – theological judgment on what the Fathers were doing, and theological reflection on the implications of the religious tradition in which one is oneself participating.

What are the reasons, other than those of method, why dissatisfaction with trinitarian theology is being expressed today? A word should be said about Wiles' other criterion, 'coherence'. Here it is Lampe who confesses most explicitly to doubts about the coherence of the doctrine of the Trinity, especially where, with Leonard Hodgson, the 'social analogy' is pressed, and real relations are postulated within the deity. Lampe cannot see how this can be anything other than tritheism. But that betrays a strange insensitivity to the christian tradition. There is no question of christian trinitarian belief involving belief in three gods. As I have argued elsewhere,[5] in trinitarian theology we are speaking of the internal self-differentiation of the one infinite source of all created being. Relations within the Blessed Trinity are not external relations. I shall insist below that we have to postulate relation *in* God if we are to make sense of the relation of God incarnate to God the Father, and also if we are to make sense of central christian affirmation that God is love. This means that we cannot possibly model our understanding of a personal God on an isolated individual. But neither can we model it, equally anthropomorphically, on two or three such individuals externally related. The accusation of tritheism betrays such an anthropomorphic conception of one's opponents' views. It does not begin to do justice to the careful trinitarian theology characteristic of the mainstream christian tradition. St Thomas Aquinas, for example, combines in a most creative way the insights of the 'psychological analogy', suggestive of internal self-projection, and the 'social analogy', suggestive of real subsistent relations in God.[6] If we find such theology incoherent, we must ask ourselves, before we reject it, whether we are not ourselves in bondage to an over-literal, anthropomorphic, picture of what the other is trying to say.

I am not suggesting that it is easy to articulate an understanding of God in Trinity. It is, of course, even more difficult for us today to do this than it was for our predecessors in the Faith. Aquinas could simply assume the doctrine as authoritatively given, and then spell out its rationality and force. He performed the latter task with unparalleled acuteness. But *we* must at the same time make the case for thinking in trinitarian terms at all. We cannot just assume it as something given. Leonard Hodgson grasped this problem with admirable forthrightness, but no one should underestimate its difficulty. We should remember that we are letting christian experience of Christ and the Spirit drive us on to postulate something strictly inaccessible to finite human minds, something about the infinite transcendent life of God in its fullness and richness of love given and love received, a mystery which we cannot and ought not to presume to be able to articulate precisely. Yet the fact that we, unlike our predecessors, have to argue the case for trinitarian belief, as well as spell out its rationality, has at least this advantage: it enables us to see more clearly the crucial features of christian experience that led to trinitarian belief in the first place, and still sustain it today. To my mind there are three such crucial features, which require us to resist the slide towards unitarianism. They are 1) recognition of the divinity of Christ, of Christ as alive with the life of God, and as manifesting through his relation to the Father the inner relation of love given and love received in God; 2) recognition that the Spirit of God in our hearts is not a matter of undifferentiated divine immanence, but rather of one who gathers us up into God's own inner life and inner dialogue; and 3) recognition that God *is* love, not just that he loves us, but that love – and that means love given and love received – is of the essence of his inner being.

I note this threefold recognition, as well as admission of the difficulty of articulating it much further, in Professor C. F. D. Moule's recent study, *The Holy Spirit*.[7] Moule somewhat ruefully quotes Lampe's disparaging remarks about the traditional technical terminology of 'generation' and 'procession' in the Trinity. (Aquinas, incidentally, speaks of two 'processions', differentiating the 'generation' of the Son from the 'spiration' of the Spirit.) Well, maybe we can sit fairly lightly to this terminology. But there was no harm in the early Fathers and their successors having invented labels for the twofold self-projection of God, which Christians have discerned as lying behind their twofold experience of Christ and the Spirit.

Let us now turn to the second of my questions to Professors Wiles and Lampe. How adequate are their non-trinitarian concepts of God? What is lost when we cease to think in trinitarian terms? In the article referred to in note 5, I suggested that Wiles' concept of God is that much vaguer, the more he retreats from the differentiations of traditional trinitarian and incarnational theology. He is reduced to affirming the 'richness and complexity' of God's being, without being able to justify this assertion, let alone say anything about it. This accusation may appear to rebound upon my own head; for have I not myself just been saying that precision is impossible where talk of the ultimate mystery of God is concerned? But christian talk of God as the Blessed Trinity is given its measure of precision, in contrast with other talk of God, precisely through the self-revealing acts which drive us to postulate a trinitarian God in the first place. We think precisely of God when we think of the love of Jesus for the Father and the Father's love for his only-begotten Son, when we think of the way God takes human life and suffering and death into himself in the passion and cross of Christ, when we think of the way in which, as Paul puts it in Romans 8, 'the Spirit of God searches our inmost being . . . pleading for God's people in God's own way', and when we think of our christian life and worship as being caught up into the trinitarian life of God.

Wiles has also, somewhat unjustly, been accused of deism;

for his conception of divine action in the world seems pale and insubstantial compared with the biblical picture of the acts of God. Wiles prefers the language of 'immanence', 'purpose' and 'presence'. Certainly, in philosophical theology, we must be careful not to reduce divine activity to the operation of one cause among others at the same level (except where God himself makes that reduction in incarnation). We have to think of the divine activity as an utterly different dimension of activity, working in and through creatures. On this score, Lampe's conception of God as Spirit has much to recommend it. Lampe is extremely sensitive to the mediated activity of God as Spirit in human lives. Yet one has to say that this conception of Spirit remains rather vague, and is certainly unanalysed. Deprived of its anchorage in incarnational christology and in the differentiated experience of the Spirit described by Paul, it fails to provide much real content for our knowledge of God. Its whole meaning seems to be exhausted when spelt out in terms of some sense of being inspired. This sense of God is common among many religions and should not be undervalued. But it is hard to see how such a transcendent/immanent Spirit can really be thought of in personal terms, especially when this God is no longer thought of relationally.

This brings me to the chief objection which I want to make against Lampe's theology. Lampe argues, in a passage from which I have already quoted, that there is no need to posit relation in God, since a God who is immanent in all creation enjoys all the reciprocities of personal relation in and through his creatures as he creates them from within. I am afraid that this to me sounds very much like whistling in the dark. If God depends on his creation for the enjoyment of the perfection of personal relation, then it seems that God is being thought of as dependent on his creation for being personal at all. And if the personality of God depends on creatures, what sort of

God is it that we are really thinking of? This is the impasse into which all forms of unitarianism are led, and it stands out here in Lampe's book all the more blatantly for the clarity of its unashamed admission. The great tradition of christian trinitarian theology stood under no such illusion. St Thomas Aquinas, writing in the thirteenth century, answers Lampe's argument precisely with a homely parable. Considering the objection that God is not alone because he is with angels and the souls of the blessed, he replies: 'Although angels and the souls of the blessed are always with God, nevertheless it would follow that God was alone or solitary if there were not several divine persons. For the company of something of a quite different nature does not end solitude, and so we say that a man is alone in the garden although there are in it many plants and animals.'[8] The point is the converse of Genesis 2.18, where God, having created Adam, and despite his own discourse with Adam, says 'it is not good that man should be alone', and creates Eve to be a helper fit for him. Perhaps this is the place at which we might recall another point, expressed in Karl Barth's creative exegesis of the Genesis 1 creation narrative. There God says, 'Let us make man in our image, after our likeness . . .' 'So God created man in his own image, in the image of God he created him; male and female he created them.' Barth saw this recognition of man's essentially relational nature as pointing to the essentially relational nature of the one in whose image man and woman were made.[9]

As I write these things I am conscious yet again of Lampe's fears of tritheism and of the dangers of the 'social analogy'. In recalling my earlier repudiation of this fear, I should add that we must not allow the human side of the analogy to dominate our grasp of the divine side. If human persons exist in relation only externally, over against other individuals, this is precisely *not* the feature to be extrapolated into God. The argument should proceed the other way round. It is because Christians believe that God exists in the fullness of relation – love given and love received – within the oneness of his own infinite being that they also believe that man's individuality and externality will one day be overcome.

What then is lost from christian theism, when we cease to think in trinitarian terms? I can only sum up by expanding on the points already made. The conviction that God is love is the major casualty of unitarian theism. Of course it cuts corners to say, with Hans Urs von Balthasar, 'God *is* Love and therefore Trinity'.[10] The argument should run: God *is* Love and therefore in himself relational, the perfection of love given and love received. The threefoldness of God cannot be inferred apart from the gifts of Christ and the Spirit. But might the relatedness of God have been inferred apart from the gifts of Christ and the Spirit, simply through reflection on the love of God? Well, I think it might, given the premise that God is love. Yet it is not an obvious datum that God is love. That premise of relational thinking about God is itself a hard-won insight. It appears in other faiths, admittedly – in devotional Hinduism, for instance; indeed one often finds the Hindu god provided with a consort. (That really is anthropomorphic theology.) But the kind of basic common factor which writers on religion such as Rudolf Otto have found in the theistic faiths – the numinous, the holy – is not easily identified as love. There is too much evil in the world and in human relationships to allow an easy reading of the source of all things in terms of love. The Johannine affirmation that God is love itself arose out of conviction that the nature of God had been revealed not only in the Passion and the Cross of the incarnate Word, but in the relation between the Father and the Son. So the full conviction that God is love, like conviction that God is three in one, arises after all from reflection on the self-revealing costly acts of

God in Christ. Nor can we say that, in response to revelation, reason discerns the triunity while the heart discerns the love of God. For the *rationality* of talk of God as love is at stake. The burden of my argument against Wiles and Lampe has been that we can no longer rationally think of God as love when relational – in christian terms, trinitarian – thinking goes by the board.

The other losses of non-trinitarian religion are of a piece with this major casualty. Christ becomes one inspired man among others; and the Spirit a universal divine immanence within creation. We no longer have a living Saviour, by incorporation into whose Body we too can say 'Abba, Father'; we no longer can think of our prayers and worship as taken up into the inner movement of God's life. I am inclined to think too that a residual conviction of personality in God lives off the capital of past trinitarian belief.

Discussion has been restricted in this essay to the work of two leading English scholars, whose virtual unitarianism undoubtedly marks one strand in recent British theology. There are other names that could be mentioned as exemplifying the same tendency. But the balance must be redressed a little at the end, if the impression is not to be given that British theology as a whole has moved in this direction. Quite the reverse is true of the leading figure in Scottish theology, Professor T. F. Torrance, winner of the 1978 Templeton Prize for Progress in Religion. Torrance has thrown a great deal of light, in his voluminous writings, on the doctrines of the Incarnation and of the Spirit, and thereby on the specifically christian trinitarian form of belief in God.

In England, trinitarian theology has been ably expounded by David Jenkins, who shows how the vision and understanding of God which is symbolised by the Trinity sets us free to take love absolutely seriously. Three Cambridge professors may also be mentioned, whose sense of the importance and the rationality of christian trinitarian theology constitutes a significant counter-balance to the work of Wiles and Lampe. I have already referred to C. F. D. Moule's study on *The Holy Spirit*. His earlier lectures on christology demonstrated the grounding of a relational view of God already in New Testament times, and the continuity between the New Testament and the early Councils of the Church. Sympathy for the achievement of the Fathers in respect of the ontology of God is shown by G. C. Stead in his book, *Divine Substance*. Of particular interest is his refutation of certain philosophical criticisms of the use of the concept of 'substance' in theology and christology. Finally, an essay by the Scottish philosopher of religion, D. M. MacKinnon, in the Festschrift for T. F. Torrance, may be mentioned, and indeed quoted as a fitting conclusion to the argument of this essay. Citing Oliver Quick's remark that he regarded as the very touchstone of orthodoxy the frankly mythological clause in the Creed – *descendit de coelis* ('he came down from heaven') – MacKinnon writes: 'What is the doctrine of the Trinity if not the effort so to reconstruct the doctrine of God that this "descent" may be seen as supremely, indeed, paradigmatically, declaratory of what He is in himself?'[11]

Queens' College   BRIAN HEBBLETHWAITE
University of Cambridge

NOTES

1. I have in mind a number of Wiles' essays, collected together in *Working Papers in Doctrine* (London, 1976) and *Explorations in Theology* 4 (London, 1979) and his book *The Remaking of Christian Doctrine* (London, 1974), and Lampe's essay 'The Essence of Christianity – IV. A Personal View', *The Expository Times*, February 1976, and his Bampton Lectures, *God as Spirit* (Oxford, 1977).

Brian Hebblethwaite

2. L. Hodgson, *The Doctrine of the Trinity* (London, 1943), p. 25.
3. *The Remaking of Christian Doctrine*, p. 17ff.
4. *God as Spirit*, pp. 33, 139.
5. 'Perichoresis? Reflections on the Doctrine of the Trinity', *Theology*, July 1977.
6. *Summa Theologiae*, 1a.27–43. In the article mentioned in the previous note, I did not do justice to the 'psychological analogy'.
7. Oxford, 1979. See especially chapter IV, where the difficulty of advancing from a binitarian to a trinitarian view is stressed.
8. *Summa Theologiae* 1a.31, 3 *ad* 1.
9. *Church Dogmatics* III.4 para. 54. Barth is following Hilary of Poitiers' exegesis here (*de Trinitate* IV).
10. *Love Alone the Way of Revelation* (ET London, 1968), p. 71.
11. The books referred to in the concluding paragraph are David Jenkins, *The Contradiction of Christianity* (London, 1976); C. F. D. Moule, *The Origins of Christology* (Cambridge, 1977); G. C. Stead, *Divine Substance* (Oxford, 1977) and R. W. McKinney (ed.), *Creation, Christ and Culture* (Edinburgh, 1976) for the essay by D. M. MacKinnon on 'The Relation of the Doctrines of the Incarnation and the Trinity'.

Epilogue

Christians who think seriously about the God whom they worship must choose in the last analysis between one of three views of God – the unitarian, binitarian and trinitarian. The purpose of this book has been to commend that trinitarian view expressed in the Nicene and Athanasian Creeds as being that to which divine revelation points. The authors recognise that there are several valid ways today of explaining this dogma and of defending it.

It is our hope and prayer that this book will help to strengthen the confidence of Christians in the belief in the thrice holy LORD who is Father, Son and Holy Spirit, one God. I close with the collect from the Church of England Prayer Book which was written to be read on Trinity Sunday.

> Almighty and everlasting God,
> You have given us your servants grace
> by the confession of a true faith
> to acknowledge the glory
> of the eternal Trinity,
> and in the power of the divine Majesty
> to worship the Unity.
> Keep us steadfast in this faith,
> that we may evermore be defended
> from all adversities:
> through Jesus Christ our Lord,
> who is alive and reigns with
> You and the Holy Spirit,
> one God, now and for ever.   Amen.

Oak Hill College   PETER TOON

Further Reading

Bardy, G., & Michel, A., 'Trinité' in *Dictionnaire de Théologie Catholique* (1950) with detailed bibliography.

Bourassa, F., 'Sur le traité de la Trinité', *Gregorianum* 47 (1966) pp. 234ff.

Cooke, B., *Beyond Trinity* (1969).

Crawford, R. G., 'Is the doctrine of the Trinity scriptural?' *Scottish Journal of Theology* 20 (1967) pp. 282ff.

Jungel, E., *The Doctrine of the Trinity. God's Being is in Becoming* (1976): this is the ET of *Gottes Sein ist im Werden* (2nd edn. Tubingen, 1966).

Moule, C. F. D., 'The NT and the doctrine of the Trinity', *Expository Times* 78 (1976) pp. 16–20.

Piault, B., *What is the Trinity?* (1959).

Rahner, K., *The Trinity* (1970).

—— *Theological Investigations* Vols I & IV (1961, 1966).

—— *Foundations of Christian Faith* (1978) ch. iv.

—— 'Divine Trinity' in *Sacramentum Mundi*, vol. 6

Richard, R. L., 'Holy Trinity', *New Catholic Encyclopedia*, vol. 14, pp. 295ff.

Scheffczyk, L., *Der Eine und Dreifaltige Gott* (1968).

Schmaus, M., *Katholische Dogmatik* I (5th edn. 1960).

Stead, G., 'The origins of the doctrine of the Trinity', *Theology* 77 (1974) pp. 508ff. & 582ff.

Torrance, T. F., 'Toward an ecumenical consensus on the Trinity', *Theologie Zeitschrift* 31 (1976) pp. 337–350.

Weber, D., *Grundlagen der Dogmatik* I (3rd edn. 1964).

Index